LIFE BALANCE FOR THE

Women on the Rise

MARSHA GUERRIER
A WOMEN'S GUIDE TO FINDING BALANCE

Copyright © 2017 by Women on the Rise NY, Inc.

Scripture quotations are taken from the THE HOLY BIBLE, NEW INTERNATIONAL VERSION®, NIV® Copyright © 1973, 1978, 1984, 2011 by Biblica, Inc.® Used by permission. All rights reserved worldwide.

All rights reserved. This book or any portion thereof may not be reproduced or used in any manner whatsoever without the express written permission of the publisher except for the use of brief quotations in a book review.

Printed and bound in the United States of America

First Printing September 2017

ISBN 978-0-9991297-1-5

Library of Congress Control Number: 2017910058

Women on the Rise NY, Inc. Publishing
P.O. Box 42
Valley Stream, NY 11580

Visit www.womenontheriseny.com

DEDICATION

This book is dedicated to the family and friends of all Women On the Rise. Thank you for your continued support and love as we pursue our goals and dreams.

ACKNOWLEDGEMENTS

I would like to thank my Mom and Dad, thank you for your love and support throughout my journey. Thank you both for giving me strength to follow my dreams. Without your constant support and love for Joshua and I, I could not have done this and so many of my projects.

To my brothers, aunts, uncles, cousins and friends, thank you for your encouragement and support. Your unwavering support goes beyond just a kind word, you show up when I need you and most of all you listen in my moments of crisis. I love you all dearly.

To my son Joshua, thank you for filling my heart and always making mommy smile.

TABLE OF CONTENTS

Foreword by Dr. Stacie N.C Grant

Introduction - The Journey
Marsha Guerrier.. 1

NEW BEGINNINGS
Maureen Smith... 4

Chapter 1 - Finding Balance in Life
Marsha Guerrier.. 5

RESTING IN HIM
Maureen Smith... 15

Chapter 2 - Finding Balance in Mind & Body
Ohilda Holguin... 17

REMAIN STEADFAST
Maureen Smith... 27

Chapter 3 - Finding Balance in Spirituality
Kymberley Clemons-Jones.. 29

RENEW YOUR FOCUS & STRENGTH
Maureen Smith... 45

Chapter 4 - Finding Balance in Finances
Vanessa Lindley.. 47

LOVE IS PATIENT
Maureen Smith... 59

Chapter 5 - Finding Balance in Relationships
Donyshia Boston-Hill.. 61

HARD WORK PAYS OFF
Maureen Smith... 71

Chapter 6 - Finding Balance in Career & Business
Monique Denton-Davis... 73

FEAR NOT, DO THAT WHICH YOU KNOW TO DO
Maureen Smith……………………………………………….. 85

Chapter 7 - Triumphs
Meicha Geohagen, Althea Bates, Tiffany Cooley, Nicole Littrean, Takicia Otero, Krystle Javier, Kabrea Thomas, Carline Dargenson, Trynette Lariba, Joi Grant, Yadlynd Cherubin-Eide………………………………………………… 87

HARVEST TIME
Maureen Smith……………………….............................. 128

Conclusion - And So It Begins
Marsha Guerrier… … … …...………………………………... 130

ABOUT THE AUTHORS…………………………………. 132

FOREWORD

Someone very wise once said, "If you keep doing what you've always done, you will keep getting what you've always gotten." This anthology, *"Life Balance for the Women on the Rise,"* offers women various examples of how to achieve balance using the inspiration of ordinary women making extraordinary choices to live their best and balanced lives. Sometimes just a slight adjustment can yield maximum results. Congratulations, Marsha Guerrier, on the courage to share your story and create a platform for other women to RISE with you!

The life we have is a gift and blessing that cannot be duplicated. The decisions we make daily, impact how much we enjoy each moment. From the time we enter this world the pressure is on…to cry, to sit up independently, to walk, to talk, etc. As we grow, the demand on our time grows. We get caught up in meeting our various obligations; those that are imposed upon us and those that are self-imposed. We have to decide where and how we manage such obligations. This becomes the backdrop for our lives as we work to find a way to balance how we use the 24 hours we are blessed to receive each day.

As a child of God, I operate through a very specific lens of FAITH. I have chosen with my free will to believe God is REAL. Now, I know everyone may not believe as I do but I can only share my truth with full disclosure of what fuels my action.

I struggled with fighting the pressures of meeting all the obligations life placed on me and the ones I placed on myself. I struggled with the guilt of falling short in one area of my life while excelling in others. As I felt my performance frustration rising, I had to go on my knees in prayer. After all, I was doing what I thought was expected of everyone; like the following unwritten rules:

- you must set and accomplish multiple goals at the same time
- you must keep yourself busy, because busy automatically means your productive
- you must sacrifice family to build business or vice versa because you can't do both
- you must suffer in silence because asking for help shows you are not strong

These realities just weren't sitting well in my spirit. I didn't believe life was intended to be this complicated. I am so excited that this book addresses the real truth of these unwritten rules.

In my prayer time, I started to meditate on scripture, *"Be careful for nothing; but in everything by prayer and supplication with thanksgiving let your requests be made known unto God.*
And the peace of God, which passeth all understanding, shall keep your hearts and minds through Christ Jesus."
Philippians 4:6-7 KJV

The revelation I received from my prayer time, was that I had to stop telling God what to do and start asking Him what would He have me do. I had to learn to really let my wills and my wants be lost in Him. I had to ask Him how I should be using the time He so graciously gives me daily. Now was this easy, not initially but I started to see that if I really put Him first, He would guide and strengthen me in making the right choices and decisions with my time. In the quest to create balance in my life, God gave me peace in the process.

"Time is really the only capital humans have, and the only thing he can't afford to lose." Thomas Edison

This book will not only inspire you to be comfortable in your own truth and find a balance that works for you, it will give you tangible actions you can take to manage your time effectively in five areas of your life. Everything is covered from goal setting, prioritizing, planning and assessing what things are really important in your life. Get comfortable, open up yourself to receiving a blessing, release all judgment and start turning the pages of this book with an expectation of how YOU will continue to RISE!!!

Counting on your success,

Dr. Stacie N.C Grant
International Speaker, Author & Founder
www.DestinyDesignersUniversity.com

INTRODUCTION
The Journey
By Marsha Guerrier

We are living in the age of social media and instant gratification. Everything around us is moving so quickly and it seems as if the more we do the more we feel like nothing is getting done. I'm a single mother, full time employee, run my own non-profit organization and operate a small business as a personal and development coach. My **JOURNEY** in business has been a long one. I know how it feels to want it all and also have it all, start a project and have to stop it midstream because of life's challenges. The journey to finding balance has not been easy; the universe has a way of putting what I call **SHENANGIANS** into our lives, but I've built systems to prepare myself to handle these challenges so that I continue to live a balanced life that's designed for me.

You may feel like you are **SMASHING IT** in some areas of your life, while some areas you hide from. Do you work hard yet still you find it tough to organize all the demands of your professional as well as your personal life? You are not alone. I've searched for years on ways to better myself with the mindset that it all has to be perfect, whether it was in my professional or personal development and I have finally come to realize one thing: **THERE'S NO SUCH THING AS PERFECTION**.

Yes, that's me yelling at you, and myself years ago. So, what does this mean, am I supposed to live a chaotic life, should I just let everything fall to pieces? For most people that's exactly what happens, they live life with no plans but eventually what seems to be a happy life will have you crash and burn. Without the proper systems in place I know in the past whenever I would get that unbalanced feeling, I would quit something or shut the world out entirely but that was not the right answer. Life is not about giving up entirely, it's about the give and take. You give a little more to one area of your life and take a little away from another at different times. But this takes **PATIENCE AND PRACTICE**.

As women we often search for balance without understanding or knowing what it is. The mindset that we've created for ourselves is that achieving balance means that everything is all perfect and stable. When we think of life as being all neat and perfect we eventually become stagnant and the feeling can halt a person from reaching their goals and growing as a person. Especially, when life throws you those **SHENANIGANS** I mentioned before, as it did to me, someone with that mindset will probably react negatively at the onset of unwelcomed change.

Most often people fail at having balance because their perception has always been that you must balance both sides of your life equally all the time at the same time, **WRONG**. The truth is you can never balance life perfectly, more than likely that balance may never sustain. People that succeed at life balance are those that develop the **MINDSET** of being "unbalanced" and understand that life's circumstances vary from one day to the next and they learn to conform. These successful people know life balance requires organization and prioritization.

The right balance for you will **TRANSFORM** as your life circumstances alter. What you prioritize in life when you are single will be different when get married and certainly when you have children. There is no one-size fits all way of balancing life that you should strive for, but my friends and I will share ways on how we maintain balance, ultimately inspiring you to transform your life.

As a personal and professional development coach the one complaint I hear from clients is that they can't manage to find balance and that they are overwhelmed by all that they do, usually they come to me ready to give up a major area in their lives. Almost immediately after working on a few self-development exercises they realize what they needed most was **CLARITY**, someone to support them in organizing, prioritizing and developing strategies that will enable them to overcome the feelings of being stuck or unbalanced.

Life Balance for the Women on the Rise is a handbook for women seeking to gain balance in five major categories of life. I along with my amazing co-authors will give you tools that will enable you to make significant improvements in your personal and professional development. If you are on a journey to finding balance in your personal and professional life, then you have found the right book. Be sure to use this book, I mean *USE* the book, mark it up, and highlight whatever resonates with you. Jot down any thoughts you have on the sides of the page as you are reading along so you can remember how you were feeling at the time you read it. Be sure to complete all of the exercises and come back to this book every time and any time you feel stuck and unbalanced.

I *APPLAUD* you for getting on this journey and thank you for choosing us to guide you through it!

With Love,

Marsha

New Beginnings

Father thank you for new beginnings, a time we can come before you; asking for a time of refreshing and clear guidance and direction for how I need to proceed on my journey. Please make clear my path and keep me in tune with the Holy Spirit to prevent me from doing things my way, rather than the best plan you have for me.

Maureen Smith

He changes times and seasons; he deposes kings and raises up others. He gives wisdom to the wise and knowledge to the discerning. Daniel 20:21

CHAPTER ONE

FINDING BALANCE IN *Life*

By Marsha Guerrier

Lately, it seems everyone is searching for the ultimate balance in life, especially work-life balance. Work-life balance has become an important factor for women in search of the perfect personal and professional lifestyle. When we talk about work-life balance, we are usually comparing the amount of time we spend on our professional and personal life, and the personal life usually takes a back seat to professional. The breakdown of time between the two is most often out of balance which leaves women feeling burnt down and unfulfilled. Whatever your primary occupation would be, whether as an entrepreneur, a corporate career, or stay at home mom; this will usually play a larger role of your life.

As an entrepreneur, you spend day and night working on and thinking about your business. In a corporate environment we are always searching for growth in salary, therefore, putting in more hours to get closer to that glass ceiling. As a stay at home mom, you are constantly in homecare giver mode and often don't put in enough time to other categories of life – mainly yourself.

When you stop to think about your life our immediate thought process is that life is unfair and often this way of thinking leads you to withdraw and quit. It also leads to getting burnt out, feeling overwhelmed, stressed, unfulfilled and like you've lost yourself. Then you begin to question if what you are doing is the right thing for you.

In some cases the answer *IS* to quit some things and make drastic changes with your life; but usually when you simply make small changes in the way you organize and prioritize life, you can begin to feel a healthier balance towards life. To make the transition to living a balanced life, I recommend you get a greater understanding of what life balance means and incorporate small tasks through goal setting in order to evenly distribute balance in your life. To begin, the easiest way to understand how to go about achieving life balance is to first understand what life balance is NOT:

- It is **NOT** having a perfect day every day;
- It is **NOT** trying to pay equal attention to every aspect of your life everyday;
- It is **NOT** trying to fit more things to your schedule in a day to feel accomplished;
- It is **NOT** something you reach once and then bam you are balanced for life.

Alright, so if this is NOT life balance, then what is it?

- Life balance **IS** a daily struggle that will remind you that sometimes you are not in control. Remember that when things start to shift, you will need to make the necessary shifts with it in order to keep in tack.
- Life balance **IS** a mindset, in order to move with the shifts of life you must have the right attitude. It's very difficult to make decisions that don't settle in your mind. You must continually evolve in your thinking as you grow. Being able to identify when things are shifting in life and addressing them immediately takes thought.
- Life balance **IS** focusing, because all the categories of your life need a different amount of attention from time to time.
- Life balance **IS** also having a clear understanding of your personal values. Your values are what

you refer to anytime life hands you a decision to make. It is who you are at the root of your being.

Knowing all of this, it's now time to do a self-assessment to figure out which categories in life you feel suffer most. I know it may be obvious to you as you read this book but this exercise is more about affirming what you already know and making commitments towards the shift. You're a smart person, I know you already know what you know but the most efficient people in life write things down, they journal their thoughts and feelings in order to refer back to them. This keeps them grounded and balanced. NOW LET'S WORK!

SELF ASSESSMENT

Rate your level of satisfaction in each category from 1 to 7. 1 means you're extremely satisfied, and 7 means you are extremely dissatisfied. I also left some space for you to write why you chose that rating. To help you rate each category I've given you questions, that should you help respond truthfully.

_____**Life**: I consider this category to be the sum of you. How focused are you on personal growth? Are you satisfied with the direction your professional life is going? Are you open to new experiences and are open to learn something new? _____

_____

_____**Mind and Body**: Do you respect and love yourself no matter what situation you are in at all times? How is your energy level at the start and end of your day? How many hours of sleep do you get, is it enough? Are you satisfied with your level of fitness and diet? Do you have positive thoughts that help you affirm the direction you are going in

life?_____
_____
_____

_____**Spirituality**: How connected are you to God? Are you satisfied with your relationship with Him? Do you use your spirituality when dealing with life situations?_____
_____
_____
_____

_____**Finance**: Are you earning enough income to satisfy your current needs? Are you financially independent? Are you where you want to be with your current savings and lifestyle?_____
_____
_____

_____**Relationships**: Are you spending quality time with the ones you love? Are your family and friends supportive of you? Are you supportive of your family and friends? Do you spend time engaging friends and socializing? Do you feel loved? How often are you expressing love to others? Is feeling loved important to you?_____
_____
_____

_____**Career and Business**: Is your career or business where you want it to be? Is your business heading in the right direction? Are you in the career that makes you most happy?
_____
_____

Thanks for being honest and transparent. Now let's review how you rated each category. If you rated a category between 1 and 3, Awesome! You thrive most in this area of your life. It's important that you maintain what you are doing to continue to thrive in these areas, however don't for one second believe that you can begin to neglect these areas in order to improve on others.

If you rated a category 4, you are not sure how important this category plays a role in your life. I urge you, begin to add goals and tasks in your life in this area for a short time and come back to reassess the category. While you may think these areas are unimportant for your survival, once you begin to experience things you often learn that it's necessary for the soul.

If you rated a category between 5 and 7, you are not very happy in this area of life, and you must put a plan in action to improve this rating.

The purpose of this was not to get you excited or get you down about these ratings, but to show you where you will focus your energy and put your action plan to work.

It is very easy to become extremely satisfied in one area, but what areas will suffer? You can spend all your time and energy working on your career or business and be a huge success. You will even become extremely satisfied with your finances because of this success; however, what happens in your relationship category? How is your mind and body and are you really enjoying all that life has to offer along the way?

The key is to find a way to incorporate all the categories of life into your mindset. It doesn't have to be every day. I do suggest that you find a way to incorporate it in life at least weekly. You can achieve this by using a planner such as the Women on the Rise Pray, Plan, Prosper weekly planner. Balance is all about give and take. To gain it, you have to be ready to make sacrifices and transform your mindset about what's important so that your ratings become equal in satisfaction NOT dissatisfaction.

Another thing to do in order to help you move toward balance is to visualize what your life would be like if it were balanced. Think about what your ideal rate would be for each category. How soon would you like to see an improvement, one month, three months, six months, and one year? Imagine that this time has passed, visualize that your ratings have indeed improved, describe how it looks and feel.

_____
_____
_____
_____
_____
_____

Now describe how it would looks and feel if you are unable to achieve your ideal rating?

_____
_____
_____
_____
_____
_____

Maya Angelou taught us, "when you know better you do better," so now that you know better, this is the perfect time to take action and set goals for each category. When you visualize the balanced life you want to live and often reiterate these feelings, it is much easier to set goals that will actually give you the results you desire. Setting goals is not just for major projects at work but it is a major tool that most balanced people use in their everyday life. In addition to creating an action plan, I use a planner with my clients where we set goals for the month, and then set weekly tasks that coincide with the goals.

Using tools such as a planner or hiring a personal and professional development coach, also known as a life coach, to keep you on track is often the key to success. To begin, set an affirmative goal statement for each category that is specific with a measure of time. For example, for Spirituality, "I will commit 10 Bible verses to memory by June."

The *I will* is your **affirmation**; *commit 10 Bible verses to memory*, is your **action** and, *by June*, is your **target**. Seeing it written will allow you to identify what you want and when you will obtain it.

AFFIRMATIVE GOAL STATEMENT

Life:
_____
_____
_____

Mind and Body:
_____
_____
_____

Spirituality:
_____
_____
_____

Finance:
_____
_____
_____

Relationships:
_____
_____

Career and Business:
_____
_____

Remember that life is all about choices. You choose where to spend your time the most, and with whom you share your experiences. You have the freedom and the responsibility to mindfully choose how you spend your time, and who you are being in the moment. The most important thing to remember is in achieving balance, you must be intentional and mindful about actually being present in your life and that it's not all or nothing. You can always choose to change your mind, just remember what's important to you. Based on the goal statements create your action plan.

Your action plan should include: the action, details of how to execute and a target date. In each chapter you will learn tips on the types of action plans you should consider, if you don't already have them in mind. Here are two examples of an action plan, one for those that like to make lists and another for those that like to organize with spreadsheets:

FINDING BALANCE IN LIFE

ACTION PLAN #1

Priority	Category	Action	Details	Start Date	Target Date
1	Life	Create a life balance action plan	Read the book Life Balance for the Women on the Rise	01/01	01/01
3	Mind & Body	Get my blood levels under control	Visit the doctor and hire a nutritionist	03/01	03/15
3	Spirituality	Learn 10 new Bible verses	Read scripture daily and attend Bible study	01/15	06/30
4	Finance	Pay off 2 credit card bills	Make payments above the minimum payment	01/01	12/31
1	Relationships	Spend more family time with the kids	Create a schedule of activities for every Saturday	01/01	01/15
2	Career & Business	Update my resume and Linkedin profile	Research types of jobs that I want so that I tailor my resume	02/01	02/15

ACTION PLAN #2

Category: Mind and Body
Goal: Get my blood pressure under control

Steps:
1. Visit the doctor to get a baseline of where my levels are
Task: Make an appointment to visit the doctor.
Task: Make an appointment to go do blood work.

2. Create an action plan to change my diet.
Task: Research nutritionist in my local area.
Task: Schedule and plan a meeting with a personal trainer

The key to a balanced life is paying close attention to all categories at all times, knowing your values, and refining them through goal setting. Keep that visual of your balanced life and don't forget it's a never ending process. I wish you much success in your endeavors!

Resting In Him

On the seventh day the Lord rested from His labor. So in this is your pattern for how we are to live. Dear God please allow my body and mind to rest in you. May I think on all things noble, right, pure, lovely and admirable (Philippians 4:8), allowing my soul and mind to be refreshed. Dispelling the things of the world and feasting on your awesome goodness and faith-fullness.

Maureen Smith

Come to me, all you who are weary and burdened, and I will give you rest. Take my yoke upon you and learn from me, for I am gentle and humble in heart, and you will find rest for your souls.
Matthew 11:28-29

CHAPTER TWO

FINDING BALANCE IN
Mind & Body
By Ohilda Holguin

Searching for health, I also found tools to help me balance my Mind, Body, & Spirit. I was an overweight child for most of my life, making it a constant topic in my household. When I was fifteen, I began to have irregular cycles and my mother, who does not have these issues did her best to help me. She took me to the Gynecologist, and gave me horrible tasting vegetable tonics she brought from the Dominican Republic. I even remember one that was made with thick molasses. None of these worked.

I was not going to stay on birth control to regulate my menstrual cycle, I did not drink either of the herbal remedies she gave me, instead I continued to gain weight. The doctors kept giving me hormones called Provera every few months to help. It wasn't until the age of twenty-one, that I even knew a little bit about what was going on with my body. After a year of my not having a cycle, my mother took me to her friend, a Gynecologist who performed an internal sonogram, and after seeing tons of cysts in my ovaries, told me that I had Polycystic Ovarian Syndrome, PCOS. He told me not to worry about it until I wanted to have children. So, I didn't. After, unsuccessfully trying to conceive both naturally and through fertility doctors, I ended up getting divorced. I know my infertility issues where one of the causes as his new girlfriend, yelled at me one day, "You're a non-making baby Bitch!"

The unconscious mind represses emotions for protection. It represses memories with unresolved negative emotions. These emotions generate, store, distribute, and transmit, "energy." Energy runs and preserves the body; however, when your negative emotions are unresolved in your memories, it causes blocks in your flow of energy which leads to imbalance and health issues.

Being overweight most of my life and not being able to manage that, not being able to conceive, lack of exercise, bad eating habits, work pressures, educational responsibilities, and my divorce, led to severe blocks in my life. My weight ballooned to 254 pounds – my heaviest ever. After not being able to breathe while walking to my car and/or upstairs was the wake-up call I needed to create balance in my life and change began in my Mind-Body Wellness journey.

Like most women, it began with diet and exercise. I simply didn't know what I didn't know. By now, I had high blood pressure, was a pre-diabetic, and decided to have Gastric Bypass – a mistake that I wish I had not made. God did not make a mistake with your body. We just must learn to understand it and love it. The weight loss surgery helped me lose 50 pounds, but now my body doesn't absorb nutrients the way it should. So after, putting my life at risk, I still did not know how to eat, how to love my body, or how to release all the negative emotions that came from years of feeling fat, overweight, and at times unworthy of calling myself a woman since I could not conceive.

I met someone who taught me about food. There is still a lot to learn, but I sat down and watched countless hours on real food. We would go to Whole Foods and Fairway and taste the difference between different greens. Salads became a masterpiece. Food tasted amazing. I also learned how to ask for modifications when eating out. My new friend also introduced me to martial arts, meditation, and pranayama breathing techniques which is Ayurveda. Ayurveda is an Indian health science of life. It offers a body of wisdom designed to help people stay vibrant and healthy while realizing their full potential. In my attempts to keep learning more about herbs, I found a class called, Abhyanga Massage, and because I had a credit at my school, I also took, Emotional Freedom Techniques. I did not know anything about either one but knew that as a Life Coach I could use EFT with my clients if I learned and the massage class for just for fun, or so I thought. I became certified in both. Yoga, which is more commonly known, is a sister science to Ayurveda which also helps with mind, body balance.

Abhyanga is an ancient Indian Ayurveda oil massage therapy for healing and detoxifying body, mind and spirit. This Ayurveda detox and stress reduction therapy is performed using essential herbal oils. It incorporates an aromatic combination of oils prepared with herbs warmed and blended to your dosha body (an Indian classification of your body constitution). A variety of Ayurveda techniques, is applied to work along the energy channels of your body, in a synchronized manner, to restore the flow of vital energy where it has become blocked. Lymphatic stimulation with essential herbal oils helps remove toxic accumulation from the body making this a detoxifying massage. Warm oil is the best remedy governing energy for healthy body and mind. Abhyanga oil massage initiates deep healing within cells. It has the following benefits:

- Nourishes mind and body
- Rejuvenates the whole body
- Increases longevity
- Delays aging
- Helps you avoid stress
- Sharpens the senses
- Relieves fatigue
- Promotes deeper sleep
- Enhances complexion and luster of skin.
- Cleans your body (detoxify)
- Corrects digestion and blood pressure and helps you to enjoy better sleep

I am still learning about this amazing science four years later, but the journey has taught me so much about slowing down, taking care of myself, and learning about how my body and digestion truly work.

The other tool I use to obtain balance in my life is Emotional Freedom Techniques- EFT, sometimes called Tapping. Tapping is a collection of self-help techniques that addresses mind-body connection. These techniques involve acupressure and mental-emotional connection. One taps lightly on specific points on the body's energy pathways (the meridians) while focusing on an event or emotion. If you stimulate areas of the body where meridians are closest to the surface while focusing your mind on a negative event, the tapping can balance the negative reaction.

Since our bodies use energy to help us repress trauma and emotions, these emotions stay trapped in our bodies. EFT practitioners like myself, help you release these emotions in your body so that you can create balance in your life. Your mind can want to be healthy, but if your subconscious mind still has emotions tying up your energy, it is easy to return to the old habits of eating unhealthy, not exercising, and not taking time to care for yourself.

Throughout the years, I began to start taking my health seriously. I have images of my paternal aunts who were extremely obese and had to walk with canes. I have made a commitment to myself to create balance in my life by first forgiving myself for what I didn't know, then learning what works for me and my body, and lastly using the tools I learned to help me lead a better life.

I am still in my journey. I say that to say that not all of us will have the supermodel body no matter what we do. It is vital to maintain balance in the body by eating healthy to maintain proper health…not wear the bikini. I am no longer a pre-diabetic, I do not have high blood pressure, and always have a clean bill of health as a result. I eat mostly plant-based foods, but most important, I forgive myself for any moments

FINDING BALANCE IN MIND & BODY

when I am not my best self. Because of working on my body, I craved to learn more about the mind, and its true connection to energy, mind, body, and spirit.

Nutrition is an integral part of how energy flows within your body. When we neglect our bodies by not giving it proper foods and exercise, it affects our organs. Organs affect our emotions. For example, the, "heart," is the ruler of emotions: joy, love, and hate. When we have imbalance in our mind and body, it leads to emotional issues in our lives and our heart organ is affected and vice versa. When we are having an imbalance of emotions, we are affecting our heart organ's health.

We usually become imbalanced in nutrition because we have not taken the time to learn about our bodies. We may know that we gain weight easily, but not truly considered how that affects all your organs or how to create balance to help it. Do you have excess cold (Yin) in your body? Some people have excess heat (yang), and others are deficient of heat or deficient of cold. With a body constitution excess in cold, eating pungent, bitter, and warm foods to stay healthy is best. Different body types, need different types of foods. I remember when I first began my health journey. I juiced a lot, became raw vegan, only fruits & vegetables, and gained tons of weight you can imagine how defeated I felt. Ayurveda believes everything is an imbalance and is up to us to find balance to remain healthy. Sickness derives from an imbalance in your digestion. However, when your body tells you that you are hungry, that is a healthy imbalance as it is notifying you to nourish your body.

There are five Mind-Energy-Body Systems:
1. Physical Body- vibrates to a third dimensional level.
2. Etheric Body- aura- memories of all lifetimes.
3. Emotional Body- contains emotions of all lifetimes
4. Mental Body- thoughts and intentions.

5. Spiritual Body- Connects our other energy bodies to Higher Realms.

When you learn how to balance your chakras, you remove any malfunction in your body, which then heals the body, and supports you in achieving your life goals. As a Reiki Master, I learned how to scan for chakra imbalances in the body in myself and others, when applying Reiki, practitioners hold a space for you to heal yourself which leads to optimal balancing.

Chakras are energy centers located in the body along the path of the spine. The study of chakras dates back thousands of years to the yogic practices and Vedic science of India. Chakras are both energy receivers and transmitters and a basic understanding of them provides us with a system of mind-body mapping which allows us to better understand ourselves and others. One way to look at chakra system is to look at what area of the body is challenged physically and see what chakra center it relates to.

Reiki reminds us that we are energy, and that energy heals the mind-body. It has been called, "hands on healing," as the Reiki Master may place their hands over your body during a healing session. Practitioners can also facilitate distance Reiki. Breathing is also an integral part of Reiki and it purifies the spirit. When receiving Reiki, you and the practitioner would pray and ask for God for your healing. Chakra balancing can also be done in Reiki. We also recommend meditation to increase perception, and disconnect thoughts, emotions from the body. As a spiritual counselor, Reiki is one of my favorited mind-body health modalities in that it reminds me that we all have the power within us to heal.

I invite you to create a new way of thinking about balance in your life. Find the tools that are right for you. You have made the first step by reading this book. Enjoy the journey to better health. You deserve it. My name is Rev. Ohilda

Holguin, High Priestess, and Associate Pastor at the Sanctuary of the Beloved. If I can support you, or someone you know please visit www.Ohilda.com for more information on all WELL by Ohi programs. Create balance!!!

MIND & BODY WORKSHEET

1. **Physical Body-** What are you doing to create balance in your physical body? What is your body constitution?
   _____
   _____
   _____

2. **Etheric Body-** How are you caring for your etheric body? _____
   _____
   _____

3. **Emotional Body-** What tools do you currently use to help balance your emotions? Where do you hold your emotions in your body? _____
   _____
   _____

4. **Mental Body-** What do you do to create a healthy mind?
   _____
   _____
   _____

5. **Spiritual Body-** How do you connect your energy to your mind, body, and spirit? _____
   _____
   _____

6. **Balance-** What is ONE thing you can do today to create balance in your life? _____
   _____
   _____

CALL TO ACTION

To create more balance in your life, I recommend that you meditate for at least 5-10 minutes daily. I like, "I AM..." Meditations. For example, "I AM HEALTH, I AM BALANCE!!!" Internally recite the affirmation over and over keeping the mind focused on your words and breathing.

I also recommend daily Self-Reiki and daily Self-Abhyanga massage all of which help balance your Mind-Body. Join WELL by Ohi Community today at www.ohilda.com and learn more about how to create balance in your mind, body, & spirit TODAY!

Remain Steadfast

Our Father, let me not be weary in well doing, rather give me the strength and tenacity to hold on until your promises and all that I am working for are manifested. Your word is true and will accomplish all that you send it to do (Isaiah 55:11), so let me stand on the unchangeable word of God always, no matter what it looks like in the natural. Let me see it through the spiritual eyes of Christ in me. You are trustworthy and true, Jesus Christ the same yesterday, and today and forever (Hebrews 13:8).

Maureen Smith

Therefore, my dear brothers and sisters, stand firm. Let nothing move you. Always give yourselves fully to the work of the Lord, because you know that your labor in the Lord is not in vain. 1 Corinthians 15:58

CHAPTER THREE

FINDING BALANCE IN
Spirituality

By Kymberley Clemons-Jones

"It is for freedom that Christ has set us free. Stand firm, then, and do not let yourselves be burdened again by a yoke of slavery." Gal. 5:1

Is there really something called, "Life Balance?" This is the question that has been posed to women since women entered the work force. The balancing of motherhood, a job or career, not to mention the millions of other things we have on our plates, has left many of us depleted and dropping the glass plates we've been juggling for so long to the ground. *Crash!* We have been burdened by a different kind of slavery these days; the slavery of stress due to our many responsibilities and the aftermath on our health that stress produces.

I do not believe in life balance per se. Like Shonda Rhimes says in her book, "My Year of Yes," balance can be elusive. It is really about what we choose to focus on at any given point in our life. And while we are focusing on that area, the goal is to not feel guilty about it!

Having a life of Spirit where we connect to something much higher than ourselves, is the only way we can alleviate the guilt of leaving our children with the baby sitter while we finish our book or having to choose to let a ball drop so we can focus on something that takes priority.

In this chapter, I will discuss ways of, "balancing," your life by transforming your stress into tools that draw us closer to the Creator through Spirit, Transformation, Restoration, Empowerment, Stewardship and Support. I will also discuss living in your, "King-dom," where your values are paramount to stress-free living.

These steps will help you draw closer to the Divine as you see to live guilt-free in the decisions you must make during various times of stress in your life. I will give you very practical tools to help you through stressful situations and use scripture and coaching techniques to draw your attention to God's divine purpose for your life.

No longer will you be burdened by the slavery of stress, rather you will stand firm because it is for freedom that Christ has set us free!

What is stress?

One of my clients said, "I don't have enough time to think about how to deal with stress because I'm too stressed out!"

She hit the nail on the head. We do believe that we are too stressed out to put one more thing on our to-do list and so we suffer through. I'd like to assure you that if you take the time to understand your stress and the effects it has on your health that soon self-care and finding the all elusive balance will come more easily to you, and your body, mind, and soul will thank you for it!

According to the American Psychological Association, stress is defined as the *pattern of specific and nonspecific responses an organism makes to stimulus events that disturb its equilibrium and tax or exceed its ability to cope*. That is a fancy way of saying stress is how the brain and body respond to any demanding situation. When we perceive a threat (real or not) our nervous system responds by releasing the stress hormones, adrenaline and cortisol. These hormones help our bodies get ready for emergency action when we are afraid. In today's society, we seem to always be ready for action and that also means is that if we do not have time for recovery and healing, our bodies will be in a state of constant and heightened re-action and we will suffer consequences.

Here are a few reasons for stress. Do any of these stresses sound familiar to you?

- Divorce
- Relationship Problems
- Ongoing work issues
- Financial stress
- Moving
- Death and other losses
- Educational stress
- Unemployment and underemployment
- Illness
- Loneliness
- (Fill in the blank)

I am sure you can see how this list can go on and on. So, how do you relieve the stress of the continuous changes that consistently happen around you? Change is all about an act of substituting one behavior for another. So, I wonder if we can alter our views of stress and turn it into STRESS! Yes, *S.T.R.E.S.S.* **Spirit, Transformation, Restoration, Empowerment, Stewardship and Support!**

What if we could view the *stress of change* as an opportunity for transformation or modification and "STRESS FREE-DOM"?

What is "STRESS FREE-DOM"?

It's your Kingdom, ok your Queen-dom! In the Bible it talks about the Kingdom of God. The word, "kingdom," here means, "reign." It is where God's laws are obeyed because God is King.

In order to better understand, just think about the little kingdoms that we set up every day. I'm sure we have all heard or said, "My house, my rules," or, "I'm the Queen of the castle." My family has realized over the years that at 10 pm (in order for me to wind down from the day) I head upstairs to my queendom called the bedroom and my throne called my bed, and all manner of business is conducted from my throne thereafter. If I am hungry, I'll snack, in my authority. If I want to watch television I will do so in my realm. If conversations need to be had everyone knows where I will be. If work still needs to be done, it is done from my throne. It is my kingdom. My rules. My territory. I reign in my kingdom, until my husband comes up stairs and then I need to share, but that's another story. It is my kingdom in my head.

We all have these little kingdoms. I have a friend whose car is her kingdom. She has food, papers, clothes and no telling what else in her kingdom. I can complain and have complained, but it is what it is…it is her kingdom. She knows where everything is whenever she needs it and when I need to sit in the passenger side she just removes the pile of junk for me to sit down. Her kingdom, her rules! And let's not talk about the car radio who has control over it.

God's Kingdom perfectly reflects God's character and values. It is the place where things operate the way God likes them. It is a place of joy, truth, grace, health, light, and peace. Likewise, your Stress Free-dom is the place that you have set up to be free of stress according to your values. It is your "King-dom." You reign and all else must fall into place in your stress free-dom zone.

Your STRESS Free-dom

In order for you to live a long and healthy life and to serve your family and community, you must first be renewed and refreshed spiritually. In order for you to truly be renewed spiritually, the rest of your life must correspond physically, emotionally, intellectually and mentally.

FINDING BALANCE IN SPIRITUALITY

Instead of *stress*, try STRESS FREE-DOM!

Spirit
Transformation
Restoration
Empowerment
Stewardship
Support

Spirit
   Spirit requires us to stop and see ourselves and others with new eyes and connect with a power higher than ourselves. How do you connect with Spirit? _____
_____
_____
_____
_____
_____

When spiritual disciplines are freely exercised, the result is a sense of liberation from the ingrained habits and patterns that keep us from experiencing God's love and the joy of the Holy Spirit.

Let's Practice Stress Free-dom!
Quiet Time. Balance your family, social, and work demands with special private times. Unwind by taking a quiet stroll in nature. Go to places that have trees, grass, mountains or valleys. Take a hot bath, watch the sunset and listen to music. All will contribute to a closer connection with the Divine.

Meditate. Take 15 minutes in silence every morning and night and meditate on the Creator's promises. As you begin to increase your faith in God's promises, the stresses and strains of daily life will begin to shrink in importance.

End your day with gratitude. Ask God to bless your day and to give you what you need to learn from the experiences of the day.

<u>T</u>ransformation.
   The best solution to eliminate the stress because of change is to, "ride the wave." It will inevitably *change* again! We are always in a state of transforming if we are lucky. Transformation helps us mature and get to that next level. It is not always easy and sometimes it is downright frustrating. The Bible speaks of transforming our mind (Romans 2:1-2) and in order to do that we must get to know our stress well. After we do this, we will be better able to tackle the job of transformation. **Have you identified the sources of your stress**?

Pay attention to activities that:
- Drain your energy and time
- Trigger anxiety and anger
- Precede a headache or stomach-ache
- Feel overwhelming or upsetting
- Do not meet your goals
- Might be one task too many
- Are under your control and those that aren't

FINDING BALANCE IN SPIRITUALITY

Complete the following assessments so you can better understand where your stresses may originate.

What are your top 10 stressors?
(Get it on to paper and out of your head.)

1. _____
2. _____
3. _____
4. _____
5. _____
6. _____
7. _____
8. _____
9. _____
10. _____

What do you value?

1. _____
2. _____
3. _____
4. _____
5. _____

Do you need to restructure your priorities to match what you value? Attempt to shift the balance from stress-producing to stress-reducing activities. Eliminating stress entirely is rarely possible, but there are many ways to reduce its impact. Put what you value at the top of your list. We do so many things in our day to day activities that hold little to no value to us. Why are they at the top? Why not make things like family time, rest and transforming your relationships at the top? You will be much happier if you do so. What are some transforming activities you can add to your list? Try again.

Let's try this again. What do you _truly_ value? (*Prioritize*)

1. _____
2. _____
3. _____
4. _____
5. _____

Transformation is dependent upon you not giving up! It is a continuous action, so keep moving, keep trying, keep persisting. *Be ye transformed by the renewing of your mind... Romans 12:2*

Let's Practice Stress Free-dom!
- **Get Organized.** In order to transform, you must be organized. Make a list of your dreams and goals or even the things you refuse to tolerate just to remind yourself. Now, work toward your goals today!
- **Update your Priorities.** Every month take a look at your list of priorities and make sure they are still of value to you. It's okay to change them to what is important to you.
- **You Have Choices.** You may not feel like you have choices, but you really do! Now, go ahead and make them. The hardest part is making the decision. It gets easier as you dig in and defend your choices. Remember, God will redirect you if you are on the wrong track. God honors your action!

Restoration

What is your first call from God? The answer according to Watchman Nee, Christian teacher and author, is to rest in God's grace. In his book, "Sit, Walk, Stand," Nee says that our first position in Christ is to sit or [rest]. What does this mean? *Ephesians 2:6-7 says, And God raised us up with Christ and seated us with him in the heavenly realms in Christ Jesus, in order that in the coming ages he might show the incomparable riches of his grace, expressed in his kindness to us in Christ Jesus. For it is by grace you have been saved, through faith—and this is not from yourselves, it is the gift of God— not by works, so that no one can boast.*

Our first call from God is to rest in God's grace much like when we were born and could do nothing for ourselves. Christian life begins much like our natural lives. We are birthed, we are fed, and pampered. We are taken care of by the grace of someone else. We depend on another being and allow that being to do the work for us. In the same way, we have been given God's grace and must remember to sit still and know that God is God. (Psalm 46:10, NIV)

Being seated is a passive position. We must learn to take things a bit slower and when we do need to work we must allow plenty of time to get things done. Plan your schedule ahead of time so you don't feel the pressure of stress and recognize that you can only do so much in a given period.

We are always on the run. We have many things that fill our calendars and we are always looking at our watches, clocks, or phones to see where we are supposed to be next. I hear that we New Yorkers are famous for this. We must learn again to be like babies who know how to rest. When a baby is tired they sleep. It is only when they begin to grow that they learn to fight their sleep. If we can't revisit this beautiful time in our history then maybe you can "remember the Sabbath day and keep it holy" (Exodus 20:8-11) It's is God's law for those who love God.

Let's Practice Stress Free-dom!
- **Take a Nap.** Naps are not just for toddlers! Science has shown that naps can help the brain restore and refresh itself, just in the span of 15 or 20 minutes. Adults regularly miss out on a solid night's sleep, so a nap is the best bet to feel energized and refreshed.
- **Breathe Break.** Take mini-breaks. Sit down and get comfortable. Take in a deep breath; hold it; and then exhale very slowly. Let your shoulders fall away from your ears. Smile and say something positive. We often take shallow breaths that do nothing to slow us down. If you take a deep breath it will settle your body and slow down its functions and relieve anxiety.

- **Relax**. Exercise techniques such as yoga help with a relaxation response that opposes the stress responses we frequently experience.
- **Own a Pet.** Research finds that pet owners have a lower blood pressure increase in response to stress than people who do not own pets.

Name some ways you will honor your first call to <u>R</u>est.

1. _____
2. _____
3. _____
4. _____
5. _____

<u>Empowerment</u>

There are so many ways that you can empower yourself, but often we are too busy to even think about the things around us that can help us de-stress. Below you will find a list of ways to empower yourself to lessen your stress.

One key step to empowerment in stressful times is to know everything there is to know about the situation. You must empower yourself with knowledge in order to be able to cope more successfully. For example, if you are having a surgery, to know how long the recuperation time will be, what at-home help you may need or how much pain you will experience will empower you to cope and heal more easily. If you are not armed with any information, the less able you will feel to handle the situation.

Let's Practice Stress Free-dom!
- **Assert Yourself.** Ask questions you need answers to. Learn to say No or Yes so you don't end up resenting people for the decisions you've made. Set realistic boundaries and respect your time and energy so others will do the same.
- **Give your personal touch to everything.** Be creative, be unique, and give your heart to everything you do.
- **Seek out, but do not deplete energy in others.** Hang around those whose enthusiasm is contagious!
- **Praise/Gratitude Break (free):** Every hour, pause and show gratitude for your surroundings and having made it through that portion of your day.
- **Use Humor.** Laugh at yourself. You are hilarious! Laughter not only releases the tension of pent-up feelings and helps a person maintain perspective, but it also appears to have actual physical effects that reduce stress hormone levels.
- **Music and Art.** Music is an effective stress reducer in both healthy individuals and people with health problems. Research finds that listening to soothing music can decrease blood pressure, heart rate, and anxiety levels in heart patients.
- **Expose Yourself.** No, not in that way! Expose yourself to at least one new thing each week.
- **Stop Multitasking and Delegate.** Prioritize and do one thing at a time, and if at all possible give it to someone else to do!

These are just a few ways to empower yourself in your new Stress Free-dom!

FINDING BALANCE IN SPIRITUALITY

<u>S</u>tewardship
The word, "steward," is found in *Luke 16:1 There was a certain rich man, which hired a steward to handle his affairs.* So what do stewards do? Stewards manage.

We do not own our bodies, but we are responsible for them. *Do you not know that your bodies are temples of the Holy Spirit, who is in you, whom you have received from God? You are not your own (1 Cor. 6:19)* We are only managers of our lives. Are you being a good steward over your life? How about your body? Your mind? Your soul? How are you handling your affairs?

Luke 16:10-15 says, *Whoever can be trusted with very little can also be trusted with much, and whoever is dishonest with very little will also be dishonest with much. So if you have not been trustworthy in handling worldly wealth, who will trust you with true riches? And if you have not been trustworthy with someone else's property, who will give you property of your own?* In this particular instance, the writer is speaking about wealth, but we can also see the correlation if we talk about our body, mind and soul. We must be good stewards of them and faithful for what we have so God will honor and increase our wealth in those areas.

How can you manage your life better in the future?

Let's Practice Stress Free-dom!
- **Meditation.** Each day, spend at least a brief time imaging prayer for the healing and wellness of your body and the bodies of others you care about. Visualize yourself and them enveloped in God's loving arms. Ask for guidance about new ways to glorify God in your body and to respect both your own body and those of others as temples of God.
- **Exercise and a Healthy Diet.** Physical activity has always provided relief from stress and a well-

nourished body is better prepared to cope with stress. Start your day with a healthy breakfast, reduce your caffeine and sugar intake, and cut back on alcohol and nicotine.

Support

A strong network of supportive friends and family members can be an enormous buffer against life's stressors. On the flip side, the more lonely and isolated you are, the greater your vulnerability to stress.

- Partner up and do things together
- Express your feelings with a friend, coach, therapist, or pastor
- Journal your feelings -"Writing down the Soul," by Janet Connor will help you.
- Don't wait to come across a support group, form your own!
- Be a good friend and be trustworthy
- Establish or strengthen a network of friends at work and at home.

Nothing contributes more to chronic stress than emotional disconnection from ourselves and others. The lack of an established network of family and friends predisposes a person to stress disorders and stress-related health problems, including heart disease and infections. Older people who maintain active relationships with their adult children are buffered against the adverse health effects of chronic stress-inducing situations, such as low income or lower social class. This may be because people who live alone are unable to discuss negative feelings to relieve their stress.

Let's Practice Stress Free-dom!

- **Worship.** Join a worshipping community. You can also find them online, but there is nothing like sitting

next to someone and sharing their energy for the Divine.
- **Join a Support Group.** Members of support groups can share experiences that can lead to healing. It is important to share feelings and resources when you are experiencing changes in life.
- **Social Media.** It is good for something! Begin a Facebook page for like-minded people who have the same goals as you!
- **Begin your own Support Group.** Why wait for a support group to arise that you can attend when you can begin your own? Find one other person to begin your group. You can find people going through the same issues and begin your healing process together.

I pray that you are able to turn your stress into STRESS-FREE-DOM using the Spirit, Transformation, Empowerment, Stewardship and Support Techniques! Remember that your "King-dom" will only be what you make of it. May God continue to bless you on your journey!

Works Cited
American Psychological Association, 2016.
Connor, Janet. Writing down the Soul. San Francisco: Canari Press, 2008.
(New International Version, Gal. 5:1; Romans 12:2; Ephesians 2:6-7; Psalm 46:10;
 Exodus 20:8- 11; Luke 16:1; Luke 16:10-15)
Rhimes, Shonda. Year of Yes. New York: Simon & Schuster, 2016

Renew Your Focus and Strength

Heavenly father, what a glorious time to pause and give thanks as I renew my focus and strength for the coming season. As I reflect on all that you have taught me and the many ways you have demonstrated your love for me, I am humbled and ready to continue to live a life that gives you praise. Please show me your ways that will lead me to walking in the plans and purposes you have ordained for my life; plans to prosper me and do good (Jeremiah 29:11). I pray for strength to continue on in Jesus Name.

Maureen Smith

Even youths grow tired and weary, and young men stumble and fall; 31 but those who hope in the Lord will renew their strength. They will soar on wings like eagles; they will run and not grow weary, they will walk and not be faint.
Isaiah 40:30-31

CHAPTER FOUR

FINDING BALANCE IN *Finances*

By Vanessa Lindley

Growing up with a bifurcated financial view of the world has left me with a constant yearning to seek balance. As a young child my sister and I were considered the "rich" cousins because my sister and I had our own room, beds, plenty of toys, a library of books and encyclopedias, we took dance lessons, were in Girl Scouts, went to Broadway shows, had birthday parties, and the best Christmases. Then at the age of 12, that all changed. We were evicted from our apartment and had to move into the projects with our maternal grandmother, aunts, uncles and cousins. This was a traumatic experience for us, times were hard, food was scarce and everyone was living on the edge. We lived there for about three years and then went to live with my paternal grandmother who owned a three unit building where she rented out two units and cleaned homes to take care of us. My sister and I went back to having our own room, plenty of food to eat and *enough*.

This life experience taught me a lesson on money very early, leaving me with a lifelong feeling of, "financial insecurity." I experienced abundance, lack, and somewhere in between. I learned to budget my money no matter what because I had to make sure I was secure. Feeling like a rug has been pulled out from under you causes you to take precautions with every step. In my first year of college, I remember budgeting my money down to the last day of classes, having just enough to buy snacks for the car ride home.

My experiences led me into a career in finance. My first job out of college was with an insurance and financial services company, so I learned about money, how to make it and how to protect it. I worked my way through the company ultimately running my own agency, winning top insurance and financial services sales and service awards. I bought my first home before I turned 30, and have owned and managed four properties since. The agency I ran was in one of the richest counties in the U.S. and I was helping wealthy people manage their assets. Three years into it, it hit me that I needed to help those with less information, access and assets to learn about money, how to manage, accumulate and protect it. So, I left the company and started my own consultant company, teaching, writing and coaching around personal finance.

Through my financial work, I've come across so many people who are successful, educated, own businesses, but still can't get this personal finance thing together. People are busy trying to balance different areas of their lives, stressed and don't have the knowledge or time to focus on their finances.

When I was a young single adult, I had a good grip on my finances, making sure I had a good balance. My first home was a townhome, not too expensive; I had my six months emergency savings in the bank, traveled the world, had a decent wardrobe and consistently put money away for retirement. I remember wanting a luxury car, so I rented a room in my 3-bedroom townhouse to cover the cost of my Mercedes Benz. Strategy, balance and focus were the keys to success.

I teach people that you must plan, pay attention and spend time with your money in order to do well in this area. Your relationship with your money is one of the longest-term relationships you'll ever have and you have to nurture it like other relationships in order to be successful.

Legacy

Start with the end in mind. The first step is to figure out what you want and what financial success looks like to you: A large bank account? A big house? Vacations? Fancy wardrobe? Extremely wealthy people tend to plan their finances for generations; middle class people tend to plan for retirement and think about money from month to month or paycheck to paycheck.

What do you want for your future generations? What do you want your financial life to look at the end of your life? What will retirement be like? Vacation home? Traveling the world? House in the country? Apartment in the city? You have to identify what you want and start planning around your goals. Set your goals and be specific. You must quantify what your goals will cost and what the target date to reach them will be. Remember, "A financial goal without a dollar and a date is a dream."

Regardless of your financial goals, there are a few key areas you must focus on to achieve balance in your finances:

- Cash Flow (positive)
- Net Worth (positive)
- Your Relationship with Money

Cash Flow

You want to insure that you are cash flow positive, which means you are bringing in more income than your expenses. The first step in achieving this is to assess your cash flow. To start you must write down all sources of income (employment, revenue, child support, dividends, rental income, etc.) and all of your expenses (housing, food, transportation, utilities, clothing, student loans, credit card bills, etc.) to see if you are making enough to cover your basic expenses. You can use the spending plan worksheet for this as well. Then you must track your spending for two to four weeks (see cash flow tracker) to see what other things you are spending your money on that you are not aware of.

Once you've tracked your spending, pay attention to trends and patterns and decide what fits into your life goals and stop doing what doesn't. You may need to cut some things out or find ways to bring more money in. Remember it is all about balance, enjoying your life today while preparing for your future.

Net Worth

The next area you want to make sure you are paying attention to and having balance in is your net worth (see net worth statement). Your net worth is the difference between your assets (what you own) and your liabilities (what you owe). You want to make sure you stay in the black (positive) vs. in the red (negative). There are times when it may be difficult to be in the black, like when you first buy your home and have a mortgage or when you first start a business and have a business loan. The key to maintaining balance in this area is to consistently save money in your emergency fund, retirement account, designated goal accounts, other investment vehicles (real estate, stocks, bonds, businesses) and keep consumer debt to a minimum.

Keep in mind that over your lifetime you will have ups and downs in your finances due to a myriad of circumstances. It was definitely easier for me to manage and control my money when I was single. Now that I am married with kids and a business owner, we have to work harder to be mindful of our spending and to stay in the black. Some people think having two incomes will make everything better, in theory this can be true, but you are now combining two different people's spending habits and if you add children, it becomes even more difficult. The key to success is planning as a couple and family, having regular meetings (2-4 times per month) to monitor cash flow, goals and upcoming events that require money.

Once you've identified your goals, determined your cash flow and net worth, you then have to align your decisions

and behaviors to reach those goals. My husband I and I did this activity in our dining room last year, where we had three large sheets of paper on the wall in our dining room
1. Ultimate Goals
2. Net Worth
3. Needs vs. Wants.

I left it on the wall for about two weeks, so everyone who visited had to see it. One of the most questioned items on the wants vs. needs list was, "hair weave." I had to include it because it can be expensive and I have to remind myself that it's not a necessity. The other item that struck a cord with my husband was private school. I put it in the want category, although it is of high value to us. The reality is, our children can attend public school if our finances did not allow us to pay their tuition. I teach my clients how to do this activity because it can be powerful for couples and families to find a balance to meet the needs of the individuals while working on collective goals.

Lastly, achieving your goals and sticking to your financial plans will require a budget (yes, that B word) or a spending plan, clearly distinguishing between wants and needs, making conscious spending decisions and spending time with your money.

Your Relationship with Money

A lot of our spending is unconscious, meaning we have no idea why we are even buying or consuming the items we are. Some financial decisions and behaviors are often based on a set of unconscious beliefs, or **money scripts** concerning money and life that may be inaccurate, incomplete, rooted in painful circumstances, like mine, or seriously flawed in other ways. For people with such scripts, following them can keep them stuck in financial chaos and struggle.

Common Money Scripts
"Money is bad… the root of all evil."

"Money is unimportant."
"God will provide."
"I don't deserve money."
"I don't make enough."
"There will never be enough."
"More money will make things better"

Common Out-of Control Behaviors
- Overspending
- Excessive or chronic debt
- Obsession
- Hoarding
- Enabling family members
- Sabotaging financial plans
- Misrepresenting financial status
- Work compulsion

Creating a healthy relationship with money is emotional work, not financial work, and often involves the following stages of transformation:

1. Emerging from denial and identifying money scripts
2. Exploring and healing repressed emotions around the most entrenched scripts
3. Obtaining new information
4. Contemplating the future (*what would I gain?*)
5. Taking action

FINDING BALANCE IN FINANCES

Assessing Your Money Habits & Beliefs

1. Where do your money habits and beliefs come from? (Upbringing, Culture, Faith, Personal Experiences, Education)

   _____
   _____
   _____

2. Are your habits and beliefs serving you well? Helping you reach your goals? (Determine Hourly Wage x Time You spend = Money)

   _____
   _____
   _____

3. What can you do or how can you begin to change the money habits and beliefs that are not serving you?

   _____
   _____
   _____

Transforming Your Relationship with Money

You can stop living paycheck to paycheck, "robbing Peter to pay Paul," feeling overwhelmed by it all and find balance with the help of a **financial coach**. Bringing consciousness to your financial affairs and engaging a mindset of growth and power can transform your financial life. This is ongoing work, I am constantly working on getting this money thing right, not letting my past control my future and making sure I protect myself and my family through healthy financial behaviors and when I get off track, I jump right back on.

Use these tools as a way to get started

LIFE BALANCE FOR THE WOMEN ON THE RISE

Daily Cash Flow Tracker

Name: _____**Date:** _____

Date	Description	Amount	Cash	Credit	Debit	Need	Want
12/1/16	Latte	4.50	x				x
Total Expenses							

FINDING BALANCE IN FINANCES

Budget Calculator
Name:_____Date: _____

Step 1: Identify Income Sources		
Source	Expected per month	Actual per month
After-tax income		
After-tax income from spouse's income		
Tips, bonuses, cash from hobbies		
Unemployment compensation		
Social Security or Supplemental Security Income		
Public assistance		
Child support		
Other		
Other		
Total Monthly Income		

LIFE BALANCE FOR THE WOMEN ON THE RISE

Step 2: List Expenses		
Source	Expected per month	Actual per month
Rent/mortgage payment		
Utilities (light, gas, electric, heat)		
Savings		
Cell phone (all features)		
Home maintenance (cleaning, repairs, etc.)		
Groceries		
Car payment, gasoline, parking		
Bus/train fare		
Insurance (car, homeowner's, life)		
Tuition or school-related fees		
Childcare & activities		
Child support, alimony, spousal maintenance		
Union/organization dues		
Pets (all costs – vet, grooming, food, etc.)		
Credit cards		
Clothes/uniforms		
Snacks/meals eaten out		
Personal (toiletries, hair, nails, etc.)		
Entertainment		
Charitable donations		
Savings for emergencies		
Savings for long-term goals		
Other		
Total Monthly Expenses		
Step 3: Compare Expected Income and Expenses		
Expected monthly income	$	
(minus) expected monthly expenses	-$	
Discretionary income	$	

FINDING BALANCE IN FINANCES

Net Worth Calculator

Name: _____ Date: _____

Assets		Liabilities	
Cash		**Loan Balances**	
Checking accounts		Mortgage loan	
Savings accounts		Home equity loan	
CD's (Certificates of Deposit)		Auto loan	
Money market account		Student loan	
Life Insurance (cash surrender value)		Loan on life insurance	
Other cash		Money owed to others	
Investments		**Other Outstanding Debt**	
Securities (stocks, bonds, mutual funds)		Credit card debt	
Treasury Bills		Unpaid taxes	
Other Investments		Other liabilities	
Property		**Total Liabilities**	
Real Estate (market value)			
Automobile (present value)			
Bullion (silver, gold)			
Jewelry, Art & Collectibles			
Other property			
Retirement			

LIFE BALANCE FOR THE WOMEN ON THE RISE

Retirement accounts (IRA, 401k)			
Employer pensions ($/month * 240)			
Social Security ($/month * 240)			
Other assets			
Total Assets			
Net Worth (Assets – Liabilities)			

Contact Vanessa Lindley:
Website: LindleyConsultingGroup.com
Email: Vanessa@LindleyConsultingGroup.com
IG: FB: Twitter: @VanessaLindley

Love is Patient

Father, I desire to adhere to you wholly; and you say love is patient and love is kind. Help me to extend these attributes to myself as well as others. Let me see with spiritual eyes. Let me see how much you love and extend your patience to me. Then allow me to offer it to others with the same grace and love that others will see Christ in me.

Maureen Smith

Love is patient, love is kind. It does not envy, it does not boast, it is not proud. 1 Corinthians 13:4

CHAPTER FIVE

FINDING BALANCE IN
Relationships

By Donyshia Boston-Hill

Your journey as a woman is one of the toughest jobs in the world, one you should never experience alone. I am honored to share my journey with you as a, "Woman On the Rise," seeking life balance as you focus on relationships. I hope my words contribute to your growth so you can build your story, legacy, and navigate meaningful relationships that will contribute to your growth. We'll bid adieu to myths as we navigate a path to greatness as you try to find balance. I don't pretend to have all the answers, but I will try to fill you with real-life advice to help you deal with the pressures of life balance. There are essential tips and strategies every woman should keep in a lockbox and access during her journey for information, inspiration, and those ah-ha moments you will have in life. Let's discover and explore why you should love yourself as you prioritize between career, ambition and lifestyle from children, health, family, and leisure time. You are worth every word I share because you're a woman, beautiful inside and out, special in different ways and we are all similar in more ways than you may believe.

It is generally said that life experiences and relationships mold you into the woman you are. I move at a fast pace but promised myself to step back and enjoy the roses, mentor, and guide woman around me. I spent several decades climbing the ladder in Corporate America, placing career and ambition in front of everything in life. That's what I was focused on, career first and motherhood later. One day, I realized time was ticking and I was no longer that young undergrad student. I woke up looked at my life, my career was growing and I wanted a husband and children. I wanted to be superwoman in the office and a loving mother, wife and friend at home. Therefore, I set out to have it all. Now, that's enough about me.

Let's discover and explore a few tips I've outlined just because you're a Woman on the Rise. Throughout my life I have heard people state, "You Can't Have It All." I'm here to tell you, as a woman you hit the gene pool jackpot, and with the right team and support system the impossible is possible if you set the bar. By setting your own ranking system you control your destiny, you set the standard and only you can adjust your life goals and be okay with the level you reach. Being a woman is an awesome experience. Learning to balance life, relationships, and womanhood means you can accomplish your dream and have it all. In our modern day you shouldn't have to give up your dreams, but yes, it's about balance.

Let's jump into finding that balance. Have you drafted your 1, 3 or 5 year plans? If not, begin now and remember you will face obstacles and detours along the way. Where to begin is always daunting, create a list of 100 items you would like to obtain in life. Separate the list into your balance categories: What you want for Yourself, Your Family and in life. It's how you plan and react during the good and challenging times that will help balance your life. Draft away because time waits for no woman. Once that's set, create a list of what steps you need to take to reach your goals. Evaluate how, why, and what it will take to get there. Revisit your list monthly to measure your progress, start small and progress.

As a woman, we find it hard to ask for help. I want you to know it's ok to raise your hand and ask for guidance. Learn when to ask for help and when to open yourself up for help. You may feel vulnerable, but sometimes you need to be pushed toward your next step and into greatness by those that have walked the path you wish to travel.

CAREER

Secure A Personal Board Of Directors. You are an investment. I recommend you sit quietly and begin drafting a list of mentors that you would assign to your personal Board of Directors. The people on your "Board," should be a combination of personal mentors and professional mentors These life coaches and mentors are your go to people when you are unsure about a decision in life. They are also the seasoned people that have traveled the road you're on. They are people that will uplift you by providing guidance. Don't select your best friend just because she's your friend. Select mentors you admire and people that won't just tell you what you want to hear.

Utilize Digital and Social Media to connect with Prospective Mentors:
- Email and request 15 Minutes of their time for advice
- Connect on Linkedin, Twitter, Facebook
- Call their office and schedule an interview
- Send a written request

Interview potential board members without their knowledge. Ask questions about their life, career path and how they achieved their level of success managing life.
Insider tip: People love talking about themselves.

LOVE YOURSELF

Fitting in and being comfortable in your own skin takes years of practice. I've observed many women that will put on their "face" and try to juggle life. Then behind the curtain they are falling apart and refuse to ask for help. This truly saddens me. As women, we have been fitting in since we were born.

It's time to stop trying to fit in to the ideal image of mother, wife and friend. You've had years of practice, so love yourself and don't forget to ask for help when you need assistance.

Here's a few loving tips:
- Eat SMART. If you're not eating well then you will have low energy. As a woman, we need you to have a healthy body. If you are ill, you are no good, and life will fall out of control.
- You must Exercise. I know it's hard but force yourself to work out. Especially if you are not a fan of your body. If you love your mind, body and soul. You will win.
- Take Some Time to Think, Breathe and Reflect. If your world begins at 6am, wake up at 5:30am, mediate, think about the day and what's ahead. Map out a plan so you make the right decisions for yourself and your family.
- Define Beauty For Yourself. Stop comparing yourself to others. Be the best you, you can be.
- Celebrate Your Wins. That's a must!

Yes, even as adult women we may experience low self-esteem.
- Stop: Wishing you were someone else
- Stop: Feeling unworthy or inferior
- Stop: Thinking you're not smart enough
- Stop: Thinking you're not talented enough
- Stop: Feeling you're not good enough.

Now, look in the mirror and say,
- Hello gorgeous
- I love you
- Yes, I'm beautiful inside and out

- I'm working hard, I'm not perfect and I can have it all.

Finally, change your conversation with your family, friends and peers: Ask them to tell you something good; something new; something you don't know about them.

AMBITION

As women, we have made inroads in society and yet we still have a long road to travel. We see daily images of ambitious women including CEOs of corporations, actresses portraying hidden figures, business owners, including and not limited to doctors, lawyers and educators to marketing executives and coders.

Some believe the feminist revolution has stalled but the revolution for all women is forever growing. As women, we are the backbone of society, the engine that could, career women, family caretakers and we provide financial stability to many communities nationwide. Yes, that's a lot on our shoulders so I've coined DB's Philosophy to assist you as you are not alone and I would like you to avoid pitfalls:

1. Start your day before the world
2. Take some time for self-reflection to grow
3. Have quiet strength
4. Become a good listener
5. Live in the world of solutions
6. Never stop learning: self-made
7. Smile and have a quirky charm
8. Ask people about themselves and show interest in others
9. Pioneer, lay the foundation for future women
10. Ask for help if and when needed
11. Use fear to channel the champion within you
12. Be humble
13. Speak with confidence

14. Always plan, KNOW YOUR CASE

BUILD LASTING BUSINESS RELATIONSHIPS

As women, in order to climb the ladder of success it is essential that we let down our guard, humble ourselves and leave our comfort zone. It's a benefit to develop deep business relationships that will propel us forward. I have learned that people do business with people they know, like and trust. Knowing someone and someone liking you is an interesting dance and the first step. In this age, it's what you know, who you know and who is in your social network. As the, "Ice Princess NYC," make note that you must work closely with others to build your way to success. Present your authentic self for natural connections. Building trust may happen instantly, a month, a year or five years but first develop mutual respect. I am lucky enough to have deep relationships that were built over the years so once I took a leap into the world of entrepreneurship, part of my safety net was the relationships and friendships I built over time.

Creating success in business is much like creating success in life. Remember, your relationships create new relationships and good business relationships can turn into great friendships. Know your circle, share advice, and build a genuine network that will weed out the skeptics. Investing in your business relationships will lead to opportunities that grow into better connections.

If I can be truthful with you, smart women know when to stop being pretentious, show empathy and interest in other people. Try to listen to what people have to say, share and show sincere interest. Learn the names of the important people in their lives from the assistant to their children.

Digital and Social Media changed my life when I decided to become an entrepreneur. It is a direct result of relationships and the ability to quickly share my dream of building Keeper of the Brand Marketing and Digital agency and IcePrincessNY.com. I am truly thankful for the digital relationships that propelled my destiny forward.

I learned to be patient, selective, and watch people in action to identify shared goals and values which make meaningful connections. I try to keep in mind that we live in the world of, "big brother," everyone is watching you on your journey, and as you know, make presumptions about who you are. Create solid real world and online connections, but be strategic, provoke thought and conversation. If you are the authority and subject matter expert, position yourself as an, "influencer," and other influencers will find you. Use social media and digital to the fullest. If you put in the time and work, you will reap the rewards of a growing network.

LIFESTYLE

Being a woman is amazing. Have fun with your family, friends, and create memories. In the past, I focused on my career and found that I wasn't present and missed important moments in the lives of my family and friends. I am the Lifestyle Event Expert and have produced thousands of events and memories for others. Today, I live to create memories for myself and my family. That's finding myself and what life balance and relationships truly means. Thus, I capture every moment which I will treasure for years to come.

Having balance means juggling my calendar and prioritizing what's important at specific moments in time. Currently, it's building my family business legacy, my spiritual growth, my husband, children, and friends. I made the mistake of missing birthday parties and special occasions by placing my career first. However, I decided.

You are going to make mistakes but the key to your balance and success is learning from those mistakes. That's how you grow. If you find yourself on the merry-go-round of life repeating bad habits, check yourself. Yes, check yourself. It's always great to receive feedback from others but your inner voice and self-approval must come from within. Inside you know when you are making the right decision or a major mistake. As women, we have an inner voice, intuition and instinct that will help us in times of need. This road called *life* will have many twists and turns, good times and bad, but don't allow fear to control fate.

Here are a few tips:
1. Surround yourself with people that have similar goals and aspire for more.
2. It's God, children, husband and then the world.
3. Finding childcare is the hardest decision in the world. Every mother travels this road, find a support group if you don't have a support system.
4. It's okay to lean on your man. Although, we want to be super woman, even she knows when to ask her super man for support. It doesn't make you weak.
5. Take time to get to know your family / friends and their attributes. We can't choose our family, but since we can select our friends they should be trustworthy, like-minded, positive and forward thinking.
6. Everyone is not your friend. I'm sure you heard that before but it's true. Friends are trustworthy and realize that you're not perfect. That helps with balance.
7. You should be able to tell your friends you care about them, I'm sorry when you make a mistake, and always be forgiving.
8. Stay away from cliques, "frenemies," and build your circle of trust. As a woman, you need an outlet!!!
9. There will come a time when you are not able to connect with your friends daily, true friendship stands the test of time and distance.

FINDING BALANCE IN RELATIONSHIPS

Now let's try this Life Balance Mad Lib: Fill in the blanks

Hello Beautiful!

Yes _____ (*insert name*), I'm talking to you. You are a Woman on the Rise with Life Balance, one of the greatest inventions since _____ (*insert an invention prior to your birth year*).

You are amazing and I love when you balance _____(*verb/talent/hobby*) Today is the last day you will dwell on being _____ (*negative adjective*),_____ (*first area you need to balance*) and _____ (*embarrassing thing you did or mistake you made because you did not balance*).

You're going to start balancing life and loving yourself for being_____ (*positive adjective*), _____ (*positive adjective*) and _____ (*positive adjective*).

So,_____(*favorite endearment*) because you are the _____ -est woman on earth. More precious than a flawless diamond!

In closing, you are perfection but you don't have to be perfect to have it all. If you follow your plan, map out your journey you will have life balance. Your plan will build the foundation for your personal and professional legacy. As a woman, please listen to your inner voice and your intuition that will allow you to #SOAR. Feel free to share these positive words with other women around you because giving back is fulfilling. In the future, I hope you pay it forward by sharing your wisdom with Future Women. Now, aren't you glad you were born a GIRL?

Connect with me:
Keeperofthebrand.com
Iceprincessnyc.com
Iceprincesscelebrations.com
IcePrincessLegacy.com

Facebook:
Keeperofthebrand, iceprincesscelebrations, iceprincessweddings

Twitter:
@iceprincessnyc, @dbmediamaven, @kotbmarketing

Linkedin: linkedin.com/in/donyshiaboston-hill

Instagram: @Iceprincessnyc

Pinterest: @Iceprincessnyc

Hard Work Pays Off

I pray Father, that I not become complacent at the onset of the time of harvest, nor become weary as I await the many blessings that are about to unfold. Rather, let me be found praying, asking, seeking, knocking for the next opportunity you present to plant seeds. May it be an opening to bless another by investing in their dream. Allow me to share with them your word, your promises, and your love.

Maureen Smith

Lazy hands make for poverty, but diligent hands bring wealth. He who gathers crops in summer is a prudent son, but he who sleeps during harvest is a disgraceful son.
Proverbs 10:4-5

CHAPTER SIX

FINDING BALANCE IN
Career & Business

By Monique Denton-Davis

As Women we have many roles, we are moms, spouses, daughters, sisters, aunts, nieces, caregivers, chefs, psychologist, doctors, lawyers, coaches, cheerleaders, counselors, co-workers, friends, grandmothers, neighbors, nurses, referees, committee chairs, and warriors just to name a few. To sum it up, we are the real life Wonder Woman, simply trying to keep it all together. So, how do we achieve the proper work life balance?

We all know that life balance is a subjective concept and may mean many different things to each of us. As a reference for this chapter, I am referring to life balance as being happy, stress free and purposeful. Achieving the right mix of responsibilities related to family, career and fun. The key word is, "fun," which encompasses your passion, purpose, hobbies and anything that makes you feel good!

Since this chapter focuses on Life Balance in Career and Business. We will focus on three key areas:

1. Am I in the right career? Do I feel satisfied and fulfilled with the work that I do?
2. Am I working for the right company? Does this organization offer benefits that are conducive to the lifestyle that I want to have? Does this organization represent my core values?
3. Am I working with the right people? Do I feel appreciated, am I fulfilled or am I headed for frustration and burnout.

LIFE BALANCE FOR THE WOMEN ON THE RISE

> **Most people chase success at work, thinking that will make them happy. The truth is that happiness at work will make you successful."** ~*Alexander Kjerulf*

AM I IN THE RIGHT CAREER?

Being in the right career means you love the work that you do. You feel fulfilled, purpose driven and content. You feel that you are making a difference. There are several assessments, skill builders and personality tests which can help you determine if you are in the right career. Before utilizing those resources, take a personal assessment of who you are, what you have accomplished, and why.

As for me, I am a human resources (HR) professional with over twenty years experience in corporate HR for both profit and not for profit organizations. I have always loved the people aspect of my work. Before resigning to become a full time entrepreneur, I began to feel burn-out. After a year into my own business, I realize that I have simply gone back to my beginnings. I have gone back to the things that I love that are fulfilling and rewarding. I have always loved writing, poetry, English, speaking and helping others. As a matter of fact, I graduated from elementary school Valedictorian and gave the graduation speech for my class. I participated in Drama, clubs, student council, the school newspaper and every type of youth organization you could imagine. I was a peer counselor, a teen advocate and mentor to younger students. When I graduated from high school and went to college, I majored in Broadcast Journalism with a minor in Communications. I was going to be on the News! I had dreams of becoming a News Broadcaster. I would stand in the mirror and rehearse saying, "This is Monique Denton, Channel 7 News, signing off."

My dreams were so vivid that I could see myself sitting at the news desk and covering stories all around the world.

So, how did I end up in human resources? Well, life happened. I did not complete my education at the first university I attended. I became a mom early and it was at that time that I realized I had to get a job. My grandmother referred me to the company where she worked and I spent the next seven years there which led to my HR career. After leaving that company I looked for jobs in HR because I was familiar, had obtained excellent skills, and I was good at it. I continued to work in HR with different organizations and worked my way up the proverbial career ladder. I also continued my education and pursued a degree in Organizational Management. During my career, I tried several businesses. I sold Avon, Mary Kay, jewelry, lingerie, and even opened a boutique IT recruitment firm, "Unique Technologies."

What I did not realize at the time is that I was searching for the right fit. How many of us have tried our hands at something or changed jobs because we were searching for the right fit? The right fit which is key to establishing your work life balance in career and business.

Speaking of right fit, let's fast forward to today. I am a full time entrepreneur, career strategist and life coach. I am the founder of Embrace Your CAKE, LLC (Confidence, Attitude, Kindness, Excellence). I am a published author and working on two books. I am a motivational speaker. I am happy, I am fulfilled, I am purpose driven and I love what I do. For me, achieving the right life balance when it comes to career and business is to make sure the work you do is fulfilling and self-rewarding.

So why did I share that story? Thinking back about my childhood and all those things that I loved to do is in in total alignment with my work, career and who I am today! Although it is not easy, I feel relief, a sense of comfort and balance. Now, I want you to think back to your childhood. Think about your view of the future. What was is that you always wanted to do? What did you fantasize about? What career did you see yourself in? What job did you see yourself doing? How did that make you feel? When you think about your childhood dreams and fantasies, did you ever think of it as work? Or did you think of it as adventure?

We all know one or two people who absolutely love their jobs and what they do. There are even some that enjoy and look forward to going to work. Do you find that they are more cheerful and less stressful? This doesn't mean that their jobs aren't tough, but when you enjoy what you do there is a distinct difference in the impact it has on your life.

How do you feel about the work you do? Now think about your current career or business does it truly align with who you are? Does it feel somewhat adventurous? Are there aspects of your job that you enjoy and others that you dislike? Do you notice the difference in your emotions when working on what you enjoy and what you do not?

Work, love, and play are the great balance wheels of man's being.
~Orison Swett Marden

Take a look back into your childhood and answer these questions:
1. What did I dream of being when I grew up?
   _____
   _____

2. How did those dreams make me feel?
   _____
   _____

3. Is there any relation to my current work, me, and those dreams?
   _____
   _____
   _____

If you can dream it, you can do it.
~Walt Disney Company

How did your answers compare with your current career or business? Do you need to make changes or are you in a good place? Either way, it's good news! There is always an opportunity for career transition if you are not satisfied with the work you do. If you are already in alignment you're on the right track and accomplishing step one of career and life balance.

The very first variable in achieving work life balance in your career is to like the work that you do. In other words, having a career that fits and being in the right career.

Work life balance benefits of having a Career that fits:

- **Better health:** According to Mental Health America.net, research shows that stress can zap your concentration, make us irritable or depressed, and harm our personal and professional relationships. Stress also weakens our immune systems, and makes us susceptible to a variety of ailments from colds to backaches to heart disease. The newest research shows that chronic stress can actually double our risk of having a heart attack.

- **Improved efficiency at work and home**: Quite simple, people who enjoy their work put their heart and soul into their careers. This increases productivity, efficiency and work performance. The more efficient and productive you are at work, the easier it is for you to go home at a reasonable time. Leaving more time for family and other responsibilities.

- **More confidence:** I love this one because it is one of the CAKE factors. Low confidence not only impacts performance, but also impacts your health and relationships. High confidence boosts your moral, relationships and ability to communicate effectively. When you feel confident and good at work, this sets the tone for your behavior when you arrive home.

> **Your work is going to fill a large part of your life, and the only way to be truly satisfied is to do what you believe is great work. And the only way to do great work is to love what you do."**
> **~Steve Jobs**

AM I WORKING AT THE RIGHT COMPANY?

The good news is that there are several companies that support work life balance for career women. As the need for work life balance increases, especially amongst Millennials, companies are becoming more competitive to maintain top talent. So what are the top three things that we want?

1. A robust Paid Time Off plan (PTO) and flexible work schedules.
2. Salary satisfaction. We want to be compensated well for the work we do.
3. A great work environment. We want employers that value our contributions, good morale and synergy.

Robust PTO and flexible work schedule

Based on the many roles that we play, it is important that the companies we work for offer a robust paid time off plan and flexible work schedules. Robust paid time off plans allow us to plan accordingly when it comes to other responsibilities for family and children. Flexibility is great and provides some freedom over schedule and the ability to work from home. Paid time off allows us to take time off when needed without disruption in our salary. For single working women whose salary is their only income, paid time off is a huge benefit.

We focus a lot on health issues that may occur when you do not have the proper work life balance. Imagine being afraid to lose your job, or worrying about a lapse in pay just to care for a family member. The stress of that alone takes a toll on the entire family unit.

Salary satisfaction

Salary satisfaction for work life balance is essential for working women. It is important that we receive equitable pay for the work that we do. Life balance is difficult to achieve if you have to work two or more jobs just to make ends meet or put in countless hours of overtime. As women, it is important that we do our research. We must be able to identify if we are being compensated fairly and at industry standards. What is your company's operating budget? Are you working in a not-for-profit or a human services agency which historically provides lower wages due to grants and funding? Do you have the adequate skills, credentials and experience to be at the top of your salary grade? Are you able to compete with the best of the best?

A great work environment

The most productive work environments for life balance are environments that trust and empower their employees to do their job. Companies that are not overly concerned with set schedules, but concerned with the work getting done. Companies that encourage an atmosphere of open communication and collaboration. Companies where employees enjoy coming to work and feel appreciated, acknowledged and rewarded. Companies where fear, domination, bullying, sexual harassment and intimidation are absent. Where creativity, productivity and thinking outside the box flourish.

Think about your top three organizational needs for a successful work life balance. Use them as a guide to determine if your organization can meet these needs.

> **"The answer to finding better work/life balance is to find the right blend between all our life activities—regardless of where and when they occur."**
> **~Michael Thomas Sunnarborg, Balancing Work, Relationships & Life in Three Simple Steps**

The top three things that will help to achieve work life balance: (Examples: flexible schedule 3 days a week to care for family members, professional development opportunities, ability to work from home)

1. _____
   _____
   _____
   _____

2. _____
   _____
   _____
   _____

3. _____
   _____
   _____
   _____

> **"You will never feel truly satisfied by work until you are satisfied by life."**
> **~Heather Schuck, The working Mom Manifesto**

AM I WORKING WITH THE RIGHT PEOPLE?

The more important question is are you the right person to work with? It is very easy to blame others in a work environment that is not working for you. Putting the blame on co-workers such as, "Sue gossips too much," or "John does not value my input," is easy to do. However, let's face it, if you have a history of having people problems in every place that you have worked, chances are it may be you.

I remember always complaining about being the only woman in the room, or better yet, the only African American in a room. I remember at the very beginning of my career dealing with an incident that would have a tremendous negative impact on me for years.

I had just received a promotion. I was now the supervisor of all administrative staff. My job was to oversee the administrative operations at this particular company. I remember, preparing for my very first meeting with the entire executive team. I was excited and nervous at the same time. The meeting was off site. I bought a new suit, navy pinstripe to be exact; a new brief case and portfolio. You could not tell me that I wasn't the quintessential executive on the rise. I wanted to make sure I made a good impression. My job was to take minutes of the meeting and offer input related to administrative functions. So, technically I was there to take notes. Didn't matter, I was in my early twenties and I felt great.

I arrived at the meeting early, stomach in knots and nervous. I walked into the room, greeted everyone, and sat where I was directed to sit. As I walked into the room, I couldn't help but notice that I was the only minority. In addition, out of a group of twelve there was only one woman. I knew the CEO and had worked with him very closely. I also knew the consultant and worked with him very closely. I had not met the rest of the team. Now the knots in my stomach turned to what felt like sharp punches. I felt extremely uncomfortable, but decided to suck it up and get through the day.

The meeting began, everyone had to introduce themselves including me. I was used to speaking in front of people so that was not a problem. I took out my clean new notepad, my brand new leather portfolio and began taking notes. The fear began to subside. As the CEO called on other executives to provide individual reports, I kept hearing these reoccurring statements. Almost everyone stated how they were uncomfortable disclosing information. The CEO would tell them that it was ok and to move forward. I did not realize, that I was the problem until one particular executive spoke. This executive was blatant and stated that he would not disclose any information because there was an outsider in the room. He stated that he was uncomfortable and not sure if the information would be kept confidential and blatantly told the CEO that he did not feel others should have been invited to the meeting and refused to disclose any information.

Now the punches that I was feeling turned into a constant pain, and the knot in my stomach moved up to my throat. I kept my head down and the tears began to well up in my eyes. I refused to let them see my cry, so I did not utter a word. But the pain and humiliation was so deep, that as I am sharing this story and reliving that moment, I can't help but to tear up. Shortly after this last executive refused to speak, the CEO called for a break. I jumped up as fast as I could and found the closest telephone booth in the hotel. I have to laugh, imagining that there was a time when we did not have cell phones. I called my mother hysterically crying. My mother said you have one of two options you can leave or you can stay. She told me that I sounded too upset to drive. I hung up the phone but was paralyzed standing in the phone booth, still very upset.

Before, I had a chance to move, I look up and who do I see walking down the hallway? My mother and one of her closest colleagues.

I felt a sense of relief with an increased fear at the same time. I said this can go really, really, bad. By this time the CEO and consultant came looking for me. Now, my mother,

her colleague, the CEO and consultant were all standing around asking me what I was going to do. The CEO apologized for the Executive's behavior and then explained how because he is Jewish, he has had several experiences with adversity and tried to comfort me.

So, what did I do? I sucked it up, red eyed from crying, ashy face from crying and went back for the rest of the meeting. My mother left the hotel, thankfully with the hotel still being intact. That particular executive resigned from the company the following week.

The reason why I share this is because we as women often fear walking into a room and wondering if there is anyone in the room who looks like us. Experiences with perceived or unperceived discrimination either blatant or subtle can create roadblocks in our careers that we don't even realize are there. That was me for many, many years. Especially after that incident. It was to the point that I would walk into the room and after observing everyone and not seeing anyone who looked like me, I would immediately say, "This isn't going to work."

It wasn't until attending the Society for Human Resource Management Diversity Conference when I heard the powerful Stedman Graham speak that I began to think differently. Stedman Graham discussed how when you walk into a room instead of thinking about what the people in the room will do for you, walk into the room thinking about what value you can add to the room. That was a lightbulb moment for me. I spent years and years thinking in reverse. My focus was immediately on others but never on me. I needed to unload my baggage, and focus on my contributions and my impact. Once I changed my way of thinking, walking into a room was never the same for me again. It no longer mattered if I was the only African American or the only woman. What mattered was the impact that I would make.

Finding balance in your career and life centers around you – your work environment, the people that you work with, the tone that you set. It is also based on the relationships you develop and how well you are able to deliver and execute.

Before complaining about those that you work with, think about you. Are you a good person to work with? Achieving balance is possible, but will require self-development and evaluating what really matters. It will require having the confidence to show up authentically and ask for what you want. It will require making adjustments with family and adding in some *you* time. It will require loving yourself unconditionally and understanding that putting, "you first is not selfish, it's a mandate for life balance."

I used to walk into a room wondering if people liked me. Now I wonder if I like them.
~Unknown

Fear Not, Do That Which You Know To Do

Heavenly Father, as the winds of change come, help me to not be fearful, rather allow me to see the power of your word and how the power of prayer effectively changes situations and people. May I be an effective instrument in your hand, seeking to do the right thing, no matter the temptations that may come my way. Thank you for spotlighting my fears that I might overcome them.

Maureen Smith

So do not fear, for I am with you; do not be dismayed, for I am your God. I will strengthen you and help you; I will uphold you with my righteous right hand.
Isaiah 41:10

CHAPTER SEVEN

Triumphs

We are honored to share with you stories of inspiration from everyday women doing extraordinary things. These women come from different walks of life and share one common thing, the understanding that life balance is all about give and take. They share some intimate moments of adversity and how they "manage" to live life to its fullest. In the end finding balance means something different to everyone, so please enjoy these words of encouragement from our contributing writers.

By Meicha Geohagen

LIFE

Confidence for me is a daily intentional choice to be who I have been created to be and share my message with the world. I haven't always been confident in sharing my message on a large scale because of negative thinking. I act now in confidence regardless of what others think about me because I have learned that no one else can be confident for me.

MIND & BODY

When I think of life balance, I think of a juggling everything women do on a daily basis without missing anything. But, as with juggling, sometimes the baton falls. Therefore, I don't focus on balance, I focus on harmony. This means that the people and things that are most important to me are always attended to first no matter what is going on in my life. For me, being a mom is my most important work, therefore, making time for my son and husband is non-negotiable. Life comes in seasons, so at times we make sacrifices based on the season we are in. Most times we make short-term sacrifices for long term gains, faith, and family should not be a sacrifice, finding harmony is more important to me than finding balance.

A healthy mind and body is maintained by putting God first and then following my own Radical Wellness Solution strategy that is, the 4x1 Rule. One hour per day of self-care, one day per week, one weekend per month and one week per year solely dedicated to me and whatever I want to do to recharge and rejuvenate. You should try it, you will be amazed.

SPIRITUALITY

More than being a spiritual person, I am a believer in God, the creator of Heaven and Earth and Jesus Christ His son. To me, this means living a transformed and victorious life and being an example to others through service and authenticity. It's deeper than just attending services, or feeling connected to the soul. It is living fully and on purpose no matter where I am or what is going around me. This is a lifestyle and I maintain my connection through prayer and study of the word, self-development and serving others with my gifts and talents.

FINANCES

I have fun regardless of what my bank account looks like. I am a nature kind of girl; seeing the clouds change is fun for me, the past year and a half I have set some very big financial goals to becoming debt free. The steps I have taken are paying off all my balances including student loans. I have done this by using all my earnings form my network marketing company www.qmwraps.myitworks.com to pay off my Sallie Mae Student loans, two credit cards and on my way to paying off my federal Student Loans. The debt snowball method, tithing and compounding really helps. Pay off small balances first then add that extra money to your next. Small wins add up to big victories.

RELATIONSHIPS

This is a fun question because when I first got married 10 years ago I thought this meant my husband and I would do almost all extracurricular activities together. I have learned otherwise, and that is ok. I had fun all by myself even before I was married not having a plus one was never an excuse for not going out and having fun. I make time to be available for my family and friends. Knowing their love language helps a whole lot and prevents many unnecessary frustrations and misunderstandings. You must be ok with enjoying your own company.

CAREER & BUSINESS
I follow the motto, "God, Family Career." When they are placed in that order, everything works smoothly. Self-development is critical. Reading and having a coach or mentor is a requirement.

MY ADVICE TO YOU
Finding or maintaining harmony is putting things into perspective. Keep things simple. Valuing the people that are around you and making them aware of how important they are to you. Read. Learn from those who know more than you, attend conferences and seminars. Build community. Learn how to say, "no," without apology. Set clear boundaries. Trust God.

ABOUT MEICHA
Meicha Geohagen-Moguche is an Inspirational Speaker, Trainer and Certified Life and Wellness Coach who inspired millions by sharing her insights through her book Radical Wellness Solutions for Women. Her experience as Social Worker for the past 13 years makes her an expert who can guide you through counseling, group facilitation programs, one-on-one therapy, workshops and crisis intervention to heal and provide you the life you deserve. Her Master's Degree in Social Work may define her profession, but her mission in making every woman fulfill her purpose of life defines her work. Meicha can help you find your life's purpose, peace of mind and balanced life.

Find Meicha at
Blog: www.beautyandpurpose.info
Website: www.meichagmoguche.com
Facebook: www.facebook.com/meichainspires

By Althea Bates

LIFE

As a spirit led woman and empowerment leader, I act in confidence with everything I do because I know that God has a calling over my life to produce works and fulfill this ministry of encouraging and empowering women in areas of resiliency and self-care. I was not always this confident and I lived in fear for a large part of my life. Fear of stepping out and fulfilling God's purpose for my life, fear of being judged by others, fear of leading others when I thought I wasn't worthy enough based on mistakes made in my life, fear of people always seeing me based on my past and not seeing any more in me.

My lowest point was in 2009. God shared with me that He would allow me to experience brokenness in all facets and areas of my life. He severed ties with long-time friends, he severed ties with the person I had been dating, He severed ties with my finances being out of work for a year, He severed ties with my mobility through breaking two of my legs. God shared with me that He wanted to use me to talk with women about Resiliency and Self-Care. I began to take my physical, mental and emotional break and allow God to take control over that year of my life. I took time to meditate and pray, and He began to work on my self-esteem and shared with me the meaning of true love, Agape love, and that I was worth being loved despite my mistakes. I found my confidence in sharing my resiliency story with others via writing, speaking and talking with other women.

MIND & BODY

When I think about life balance for the mind and body and what that means, I think about self-care, self-love, and always assessing in my actions whether or not I am building time to care for myself. I have learned that unless my self-care cup is replenished on-going I can be my best self for the people I need to be around. I have also learned what it means to give from the overflow of my perpetual cup that I have to refill and replenish my self-care reserves before I can pour out to others. My work to maintain a healthy mind and body consists of incorporating journaling and reflecting on my thoughts and experiences on a daily basis, reading the Bible and other spiritually based materials, taking long walks to rejuvenate my mind, body and spirit, as well as connecting regularly with women God has placed in my life as anchors. My anchors are women that feed my spirit and pray for and with me, encourage and empower as well as equip me to continue reaching out to women.

SPIRITUALITY

I consider myself to be spiritual. I believe that we all have an innate God-given purpose that we need to tap into to fulfill God's role for our lives. I am guided by the spirit of God in all my dealings. I follow God's leading at all times as I remember a time and period of my life that I would call "Disobedience to God." It was a time an period when I acted on self and self alone. A time and period when I heard but ignored or even drowned out God speaking to me. I also remember the cost of that disobedience and the consequences God allowed me to experience based on that disobedience. Based on these experiences, I have now learned to rely on God in all aspects and areas of my life including my relationships, business, education, family, friendships, etc.

FINANCES

In thinking about balance while having fun relative to my financial goals, I have joined networks with women who like to support each other by accomplishing financial goals. For instance, I am part of a Dream Catchers CT Network of women focused on improving the health and vitality of their finances. We share tips and strategies to help us save, become thrifty, track our spending, work on our debt to income ratio. I take several steps to being financial sound including the use of a financial planner that I meet with regularly to make adjustments to my investments and portfolio items, I have used a financial coach to work out goals to reduce my debt and I have also made efforts to join partner cooperative savings clubs with groups of women that create targeted goals for savings and create a cooperative banking system which allow contributors to take turns receiving their, "partner draw." I have learned that working cooperatively with others on my financial plan and goals has been the most successful strategy not holding me accountable to myself but also to these shared networks.

RELATIONSHIPS

I have learned to acknowledge and listen to myself and my needs as an innate introvert and self-taught extrovert. I develop times throughout the week to be build-in self-care and time with self. I take at least an hour to two out of my day to be alone with my thoughts and reflect and be engaged and in tune with myself and my environment. I have found that I need this time as an introvert just as much as I need to connect and interact with others. I have found that it is necessary to acknowledge and provide opportunities for me to be alone so that when I do reconnect I am fully recharged, refreshed and ready. I find time to nurture the people in my life through carving out time for quality and enriched experiences and interactions. I find creating experiences around shared interests has been the most effective approach and this has been valuable for all types of relationships relative to family, friends, business networks, etc.

CAREER & BUSINESS

I work and strive hard to maintain balance between my career/business and other areas of my life. The thing that I have done as much as possible is to incorporate my family into the work I am doing with Project Resiliency Movement. We take what we call, "Daycations," as a family. Many times we don't have the opportunity to take extended trips, but we will discover and explore locations for a day or two and build in as many experiences as we can. I also will do as much as possible to disconnect during these times and be fully engaged in the moments being created. I also will balance out my business activities and engagements on a monthly basis as not to be too overloaded with work. The most important thing I have learned is that you have 24 hours and you have to make the things in your life a priority that mean something to you. I will sacrifice sending my laundry to the laundry mat to be done or have someone come in and clean my house once a month because that allows me the time I need for the things that are my priorities: God, My Family and My Business.

ABOUT ALTHEA

Althea Bates has worked in social services and workforce development for over 16 years. She is a Jamaican native, an entrepreneur, a professor/lecturer, a nonprofit leader and a champion for women empowerment issues. She received a Bachelor of Science in Psychology from Temple University, Masters of Science from Springfield College in Human Services with a concentration in Organizational Management and Leadership and is currently a Doctoral Candidate at Capella University.

Althea, is the CEO and Founder of A. Bates Consulting which provides a range of training -related consulting services to nonprofits/municipalities relative to topics and areas in youth development, case management, workforce development and human services practices. She currently holds the role of Director of Programs and Workforce

Development at Billings Forge Community Works by profession.
In August of 2016, Althea launched and founded The Project Resiliency Movement and The #ResiliencyConference2016 which started with a vision by the founder to support women in embracing the fact that they don't always have to be strong.

Find Althea at
Instagram: @Theaweb26

Facebook Group: Resiliency Circle

Facebook Pages: Project Resiliency Movement and Althea Webber Bates

LIFE BALANCE FOR THE WOMEN ON THE RISE

By Tiffany Cooley

LIFE

Walking in complete confidence every day is certainly something we all should wish to accomplish. While that is something I strive to do daily, I don't always live up to that desire. I can remember a time when I was pregnant with my son. I was diagnosed with Placenta Accrete. After hanging up the phone from the nurse who gave me a report that my condition could lead to me being in the ICU after delivery and even possible death, I felt completely immobilized. It was a moment that I remember my faith was on one shoulder speaking of hope and trust, but my fear and emotions were on the other speaking defeat. I can remember feeling as though I was in a battle within myself, having to pick a side just so that I could lift myself from my knees. I've come to understand that life will always present moments where my confidence may not be at 100%, but if I lean on the side of faith, I can move forward and achieve more.

MIND & BODY

When I think about balance of the mind and body, I think about wholeness. God has not created us to be unhealthy in our body, or unhealthy in our minds. Balance to me doesn't suggest that things will always weigh even on a scale, but that we should always be working to achieve a healthy stance in both our mental and physical existence. Eating well and exercising has recently become more important to me than ever before. I now realize the body requires the appropriate fuel to sustain its wellbeing. A return to plant based eating focusing on natural nourishment has become a necessity to sustain my physical health. While intentionally fueling my physical body, I understand that this is equally important for me to intentionally fuel my mind. I am attempting to be intentional about the thoughts I allow myself to entertain. Holding on to unhealthy thoughts can be detrimental to our mental health. Holding on to past hurts, doubt, fear, and unforgiveness prove to be counterproductive and paralyzing.

SPIRITUALITY

My spirituality is the cornerstone of my being. God is the source of my strength and direction. I incorporate my spirituality every day in some capacity. Because I understand that my destiny is directly tied to the direction I get from God, I pray daily to stay in communion with Him. Connections I make, businesses I start, how I relate to others are all subject to my attempt at moving in a direction that would be pleasing to God. Understanding that I am a spiritual being wrapped in flesh, I understand that I may not always get "it" right, but having a relationship with God will allow for me to hear and adjust accordingly with grace, mercy, and power on my side. Allowing myself to operate spiritually helps me to remove the hindrances that come from making decisions that are solely based on my emotions.

FINANCES

The balance of having a certain amount of financial discipline and enjoying life is certainly important. Making purchases that don't grow my business or secure my family's financial future have taken a backseat now more than ever before. My idea of fun is spending time with my husband and children. Most of my discretionary income is certainly well spent watching the smiles on my children's faces. I've come to understand that being intentional about budgeting and investing cuts down the stress on both myself and my family; allowing us the ability to move forward in our lives vs retracting and recovering.

RELATIONSHIPS

Having a balance in my relationships outside of work and family is an essential part of my overall wellbeing. I pour so much of myself out that it is equally important for me to surround myself with others that are willing to pour into me as well. I am working to achieve that by being selective about the people who I connect with and spend free time with.

CAREER & BUSINESS

I believe the single most important lesson I've learned as it relates to business and life balance is to be present at work, and be present at home.

Three tips I'd like to leave with you:
1. Plan and execute with intention, passion and purpose.
3. You matter too. Don't neglect yourself care.
3. Enjoy the journey.

ABOUT TIFFANY

Tiffany Cooley is an author, inspirational speaker and empowerment coach, who has dedicated her life's works to seeing Christian women realize their purpose and materialize their goals by awakening their unique God gifted talents. During the course of her career, Tiffany's innovative approach, results driven methods and genuine compassion has graciously guided many to the path of peace, happiness and fulfillment in their personal and professional lives. As an active minister Tiffany devotes a large portion of her ministry to helping women face the challenges of leading and maintaining a Christian life in an ever-evolving modern society. Through consulting and counseling, Tiffany compliments her spiritual approach with practical methods to educate and empower women to leap over barriers and unleash their gifts for unstoppable professional and personal growth.

TRIUMPHS

On a personal note, Tiffany is a loving wife and proud mother of two amazing children and continues to expand her reach with the mission to lead Christian women out boundaries to their success.

Find Tiffany at
Facebook: Tiffany Cooley

Website: www.tiffanycooley.com

By Nicole Littrean

LIFE
My true confidence and owning "my stuff" arrived when I suffered the enormous impact of losing my son as a stillbirth at 39 weeks. I was 35 years old, and until that point I had suffered loss but not to the point of it jeopardizing my sanity. After living in a state of recovery for many years I finally woke up and decided I needed to thrive rather than just survive. My risks became bigger and bigger and in my early "woke" stages I decided to wear my hair natural to my very corporate job although claiming to be fashion forward. The first day I almost made myself sick walking to work, but I had a much needed conversation with myself during that 15 minute walk and I said, "Self, own this! Walk tall and smile." I never looked back.

MIND & BODY
Your mind, body and soul for me are all connected and it is important to find things that nurture all of these. It is only when you have this true connection that you can own your, "stuff." For me I need exercise, I need weight training, I need intense heart pumping workouts that make me sweat, make my mind expand, make my body move, and make my soul elevate.

SPIRITUALITY
"The quality of being concerned with the human spirit or soul as opposed to material or physical things." I feed my spirituality by opening my eyes, truly opening them and seeing the world clearly through prayer and a deep connection with my prayer circle, The Sisters of Divine Grace. This group was formed over 10 years ago, and we fight our battles on our knees.

TRIUMPHS

FINANCES
I believe life is to live and the essence of living a fulfilled life is enjoying every moment. However if you are like me you have to be a "Hustler" and not everyone has this quality. If you want something and cannot attain it because of financial restrictions…make a plan, set a timeframe, and go out and get it. I am by no way saying that priorities shouldn't be set, but do not live in fear of the limitations set by your current bank account. Make a change.

RELATIONSHIPS
I was married for 16 years and during that time I learned a lot about myself. Togetherness is very important but you can never lose yourself or who you are in any relationship. Continue to do what is important to you and you will want to nurture the people you love in your life. "To thine own self be true."

CAREER & BUSINESS
My day starts at 5am, Monday through Friday. I personal train clients at 5:45am, make sure my teenager is up and leaves for school on time, and the come back home to get my 5 year old ready for the bus. At 8:08am I am on the train for a 2-hour commute to work in NYC. I return home on most days at 8pm. I manage all of this because I have a passion for what I do and I have learned to delegate. Everyone has a role to play including my kids. I am SUPER but I am not a SUPERHERO. Passion and delegation get me through my days and if I make a mistake I try to keep guilt out of it. I am HUMAN and I am okay with that.

ABOUT NICOLE
Nicole Littrean is a Certified HIIT (High Intensity Interval Training) Personal Trainer and Spin Instructor for over 8 years. Nicole's true fitness journey began over 10 years ago when I was in my early thirties and I wanted to truly make

working out a part of my life...sort of like brushing my teeth. Being over 40, it proved challenging to get rid of the weight. With the help of a trainer, spinning, a sensible diet, and changing up of my weight training routine, I was not only able to shed those 10 pounds but also add a great deal of muscle.

In 2016, I created The NikkyLit Impact to help people redefine themselves not only by building muscle and getting their heart rates up but by helping them become their best self. The mind, the body and soul are one, and each part needs to be nurtured. I am on my journey to my best self and I will continue to grow and evolve. No longer will I be defined by a dress size or the number on the scale. I do not have a six-pack, bulging muscles or a competition body but when I look in the mirror I no longer ask, "is that me?" I say, "You are becoming your best self!"

Find Nicole at
Instagram: @nikkylitimpact

Facebook group:
www.facebook.com/groups/nikkylitimpact

By Takicia Otero

LIFE

About three years ago, I became frustrated with my overwhelming need for approval. My outward appearance and outgoing personality portrayed confidence and strength, but on the inside my spirit was dying. I cannot pinpoint an isolated incident when I didn't walk in confidence... there were so many. What I can tell you about is the day I decided I was tired of living that way! I have overcome this by allowing myself to be free from the opinions and perceptions of others. I was becoming resentful toward the same people I was trying to please. As I searched my soul for answers... I realized I had been spending my life making others responsible for my happiness, then blaming them because I wasn't fulfilled. My self-esteem was non-existent. I began to love myself wholeheartedly, telling myself I was beautiful, strong, fierce, wonderfully made, and fearless.... until I really believed it. I started taking full responsibility for my actions and became my biggest advocate. The opinions of others no longer affected me, and fear no longer controlled my decisions. I am confident regardless of what anyone thinks... I'm an overcomer!

MIND & BODY

Maintaining a healthy mind and body are important in finding balance in your life. I work on keeping a healthy mind by being protective about what I allow to enter my mind. "Garbage in, garbage out," is an old cliché that I've heard growing up. If our minds are consumed with unedifying thoughts and images, how *can* we have healthy thoughts and perceptions? Reading inspirational books, the Bible, meditating, and practicing forgiveness is what keeps my mind strong, healthy, and well-balanced. It is easier to maintain a healthier body and lifestyle when my mind is free from clutter and stress. Having a life balance for the mind and body is not just about looking good in those jeans… it's about transformation from the inside out!

SPIRITUALITY

I am a born again Christian and incorporating spirituality into my everyday life is as necessary to me as breathing! I begin and end my day in prayer, meditation, and studying the Bible. I believe in asking God's guidance for the right direction in life, and when I have a right relationship with God, He will lead me to the path that He has planned for my life. I'm enjoying life by living out His will for my life. I live my life as a ministry because our lives are not about us, but it's about what we can do for others. Following the principals of the Bible is not just something I do, but it's who I am.

FINANCES

Because I am free from others' opinions about me, I don't have to live according to someone else's standards. I have learned to balance a fun life while striving to be financially balanced. My approach to life is rather simple, it's wisdom. I must apply wisdom by living within my means, and being honest about my budget. I use creativity, planning, and preparation to ensure that my family can enjoy and embrace a fun-filled life, while I enjoy being debt free!

RELATIONSHIPS

Setting boundaries is how I balance togetherness and my own individuality. I believe you can only nurture the people in your life if you take time to nurture yourself. Even if it's only fifteen minutes a day, allow yourself time to do something you enjoy doing alone. Reading, writing, dancing, whatever you enjoy. Something you did as a hobby before you had the responsibility and role as nurturer. When you feel complete as a woman, you contribute more in your togetherness.

CAREER & BUSINESS

Going back to college to complete my Social Work degree after being out of school for 18 years has been both challenging and rewarding. I have been a Special Needs teaching assistant for 20 years. Although I believe I make a difference in the lives of families daily, God has placed a desire in my heart to work with women. There are obstacles to being a full-time adult college student, employee, and parent of two, but determination is my motivation. I look forward to my children applauding on my graduation day!

ABOUT TAKICIA

Takicia is a Blogger, born and raised in New Jersey and moved to South Carolina in 2006. Takicia is a proud mother of two beautiful, smiley children, Darius (son) and Dakota (daughter). She is simply enjoying life by loving others.

Find Takicia at
Blog: liveonpurpose247.wordpress.com
Facebook page: www.facebook.com/liveonpurpose247blog/

By Krystle Javier

LIFE

When I first launched my business full time, I had a tough time addressing client objections to service and product costs. It was quite challenging, but by working continuously with my clients and having a solid knowledge of my products and what my services entail, I have been able to better educate and overcome most all objections and create lasting professional relationships.

MIND & BODY

Finding a balance is incredibly important to stay sane in such a busy environment. To me that means doing my best to maintain a sleep/wake/work/play/rest schedule during the week, and finding time to enjoy family and friends on a regular basis. This helps my mind and body recharge, and start planning productively for the coming days and weeks.

SPIRITUALITY

I am very spiritual. I don't go to church often, but I do take time out of every day to thank God for His many blessings, and for seeing us through countless achievements. I like to pray at least once a day and do some self-reflection randomly when I have a few moments to myself.

FINANCES

Financial balance is so important to my family and I. We generally take our monthly earnings and take care of all essential expenses first and foremost. Whatever is left over is divided into savings and fun activities, as well as, "wants." It has been quite easy to stay on target with this approach.

RELATIONSHIPS

I am the type of person to take care of everyone else first. Finding alone time is a challenge. Admittedly, I could use some more, "me time," however, I do find peace and calm in doing odd things like painting, reading books, dancing, swimming, and simply napping when I can find a moment. I nurture my friends and family all other hours of the day!

CAREER & BUSINESS

Since I primarily work from my home studio, I set business hours each week and do my best to stick to them. I find that being able to set my own hours is very freeing and has allowed me to become most productive. I would encourage using a calendar, alarms or notices for important tasks, writing "to-do" lists, and simply following a routine. On the personal side, I have found that implementing these calendar reminders and planning fun things is equally as important. Consistently scheduling activities for work and play is a skill that has helped mainstream things for everyday life. Something I have found incredibly helpful is utilizing my village of helpers so that I can take time for professional and personal development. That means finally taking up friends and family members on their offers to watch our little one, or letting a fellow business woman step in to provide inspiration for a new idea - something that as working mothers, we often overlook. It means taking an hour to pamper myself with a new hairstyle or manicure every so often, or scheduling a workshop or training appointment so I stay on target – doing a little of everything so the, "activity sprinkles," are well rounded. And at the end of the day, if plans and goals change or evolve, that is okay. Life goes that way.

ABOUT KRYSTLE

I started in Photography as a young teenager, as most of us have – capturing important moments within family gatherings and special occasions. I was called upon at all times to serve as the "memory freezer" and the one in charge of sending it all to print so that our elders could fill up the giant albums they insisted on putting together.

As I made my way through college, and then graduate studies, I also worked in the corporate world. I held positions working with children in child protection, and in administration at private pre-schools. I developed an even deeper love for children and families as a result of working so closely in such a wide array of capacities.

I maintained my love of portraiture over the years and once I became a mother, I realized how truly important it was for me to share my passion with other families, and provide lasting memories they could use to fill up all of the walls and albums – as our parents and grandparents have done for many years.

Find Krystle at
Website: www.kmichellephotography.com
Email: booking@kmichellephotography.com

By Kabrea Thomas

LIFE
Growing up I never knew what it felt like to have confidence in my mind, body and image. It's because of my journey, and my experiences that I was able to overcome my insecurities. I wasn't surrounded by women daily who had confidence in themselves, it wasn't until junior high school that I realized self-confidence is important-and it was something I was lacking. I was surrounded by people who I considered friends at the time who would always put me down. I was never thin, slim or tall enough. The constant battle I had with myself in high school that I started starving myself. I thought if I was thin enough then maybe I'd be considered beautiful. And the truth is, that I was always beautiful, I just wanted to fit into what my "friends" standards of beauty was. I was able to accomplish my inner confidence by cleansing those "friends" out of my life. You are beautiful and worthy. We all are a form of art.

MIND & BODY
Having a balance for the mind and body to me means cleansing negativity out of your energy. Cleansing negativity can be many things like the food you eat, the environment, the people you're surrounded by and so on. I've been able to stay balanced by cleansing any type of negative energy I see coming my way. Your body and mind is your temple and I continue to treat mine with positivity each and every day.

SPIRITUALITY
Yes, I am spiritual. I've never understood anything about spirituality until I became more focused on my business. Spirituality to me is all about ENERGY! Your spirit and energy is never wrong, I always say, "It's never about how

long you've known someone, it's about the energy they give off."

FINANCES

When it comes to balancing a fun life with your financial goals, the idea is to maintain financial stability. Of course there will be bad weeks, but the goal is to analyze why you didn't reach your financial goals. There are just three simple steps that I use to execute my financial goals of stability. First, I create a realistic goal to hit monthly, when creating these goals, consider your responsibilities such as rent, bills, mortgage, food, and etc. Secondly, I analyze what guaranteed income I have for the current quarter. If I don't have much going on for the quarter, I ask myself what I can do for the next three months that will put me and my business in a good space. Lastly, I execute those goals and treat myself to dinner, a movie or I take myself shopping. Never forget to reward yourself!

RELATIONSHIP

I think I balance looking assembled pretty well (that's because I'm an image consultant), but I'm not and I don't think anyone is. I don't think anyone is, "well put or together," whether you're a parent, college student, business woman. The truth is, we will always have a list of a million and one things to do, but it's how you complete those million and one things off your to-do list. When it comes to connecting and nurturing my relationships I always take the time out, and make sure I include these activities in my calendar. These activities are just as important as my work.

CAREER & BUSINESS

Your time is extremely important, and it's one of those things that you'll never get back. One of the ways I balance out my life is by writing down all the important tasks that I need to complete for the day. As a career/business woman it's so easy to get caught up in your work, and that's mainly because you love what you do! It's okay to take a break, a vacation, or have a girl's night out without feeling guilty. I remember when I used to feel guilty for doing anything that wasn't correlating to my business, but the truth is, you have to separate yourself from your business from time to time. It is still IMPORTANT to hustle, but it's just as important for you to have somewhat of a social life, time to yourself, a relationship, and so on. So, my advice to you is to make it mandatory that you have two hours to yourself a day. You can decide whether you want to break those two hours throughout the day, or use it all at once. Take yourself out to brunch, you deserve that too!

ABOUT KABREA

With a savvy sense of style, Kabrea's has been able to push all boundaries with her drive, ambition and determination. As a young entrepreneur, author and fashionista she serves as the ultimate inspiration and living proof of attainable success for many. Self-Motivated Kabrea started her first business, Fashionably Yours, at just the age of nineteen. After getting forced out of college because she was no longer able to afford college, Kabrea then applied to several unpaid internships to get her foot in the door. After three years of working retail, and two internships, Thomas found a new love and talent of hers – personal styling. Kabrea loved the idea of developing a friendship with her clients while customizing a wardrobe suitable for their lifestyle. In 2013, it was just the beginning of her many successes.

Find Kabrea at
Facebook: https://www.facebook.com/kabreathomas1/
Instagram: https://www.instagram.com/kabreathomas1/
Twitter: https://twitter.com/kabreathomas

Fashionably Yours, (NYC Image/Wardrobe Styling & Personal Shopping Firm)
Facebook: https://www.facebook.com/fashionablyyoursnyc/
Instagram: https://www.instagram.com/fashionablyyoursnyc/
Twitter: https://twitter.com/fy_nyc
Pinterest: https://www.pinterest.com/Fy_nyc/
Polyvore: http://fashionablyyoursnyc.polyvore.com/
Website: https://www.fashionablyyoursnyc.com/

Signature Scents by Hand (Online Custom Fragrance Shop)
Facebook: https://www.facebook.com/Signaturescentsbyhand/
Instagram: https://www.instagram.com/signaturescentsbyhand/
Website: https://www.signaturescentsbyhand.com/

By Carline Dargenson

LIFE
My confidence level is pretty up there and I'm happy to say that I rarely need validation from most people. There are times when I do question my confidence. There was a time when I was auditioning for the educational team for L'oreal /Mizani. I thought I had it all covered and was confident enough to tackle any question or demonstration they threw at me. Well, I was sadly mistaken. The doubt started coming as I entered the building where the auditions were being held and as I saw other stylists there and arriving after me. During the audition, I stumbled with my words, became repetitive and even forgot key words that I use in the everyday English language.

MIND & BODY
Having mind and body balance means that I am feeding my mind healthy thoughts and instilling prayer, as well as taking care of my body so that it can sustain my career. I feel this is very important for my sanity. I maintain this by keeping my favorite books and devotionals on my phone and read them daily. The ultimate key to mind balance is keeping positive folks in my circle and pulling away when I need my, "me" time. Time alone is very important to me. It helps me to meditate and re-group. For body balance, I make sure to keep healthy by any means: apps, various workouts, running and/or walking.

SPIRITUALITY
Yes, I am spiritual. I incorporate it by reading daily plans with scripture everyday and staying in constant prayer.

FINANCES
Being financially balanced was challenging as an entrepreneur. I had my ups and downs but finally got it

together. I always paid myself a salary but what I wasn't doing was adhering to the budget. Now, I put aside for my top two highest expenses so that I won't fall short on the very important things and then budget the rest to focus on paying off bills.

RELATIONSHIPS
I make time for my good friends or family. This is needed for my mental sanity and a great time to disconnect from business. We have the ability to create a space for all the special people in our lives.

CAREER & BUSINESS
I truly believe that there is no such thing as work/life balance. There will be an area that will be stronger and weaker. Those areas just take turns. There will be a season where you will not be the best parent because the business needs extreme focus, and there will be a season where parenthood prevails and the business is lacking.

ABOUT CARLINE
As a second generation stylist, Carline Dargenson, grew up in a salon environment for most of her life. Her first passion was drawing and sketching art that then evolved to the love of creating art with her shears.

Carline Dargenson is the face behind Instyl Haircare and This Stylist Life blog. She has been a stylist for over 18 years. She loves to educate her clients on how to properly care and maintain their hair. She is a true believer in advance training and attending hair/trade shows throughout the year. She loves bringing back new techniques and information to share with her clients. She is Vidal Sassoon trained and a former educator for L'Oreal/Mizani.

TRIUMPHS

Find Carline at
Facebook: www.facebook.com/instylhaircare
Instagram: www.instagram.com/intylhaircare
Twitter: www.twitter.com/intstylhaircare

By Trynette Lariba

LIFE
I act in confidence regardless of the opinions of others. Several years ago when we started our business, there were some negative opinions and naysayers when I shared about opening the business. This was going to be my first introduction into entrepreneurship so I was very excited. It was discouraging that people close to me did not fully understand the reason that I would need to open a business. I remember thinking twice about starting, but then decided to press on because I knew my, "why." I remembered that the vision was not given to them so they would not be able to see what I did. I knew that God would not give me an assignment without equipping me to bring it to fruition and my confidence was fully restored.

MIND & BODY
I believe that a healthy mindset is the foundation for a healthy body. We are holistic beings that achieve optimal success when the mind, body and soul are in equilibrium. It gives you total tranquility and serenity. I keep my mind and body balanced by first and foremost making sleep and rest a priority. I say, "no," when needed and do not overbook myself. I also exercise four days a week in the early morning hours. I pray and read the Bible to keep my mind sharp. I listen to podcasts that feed my mind with positivity, motivation and empowerment. I eat to fuel my body. I pay close attention and listen to my body so that I know what it needs or if any changes have occurred that need to be addressed. Keeping a routine also helps things stay balanced.

SPIRITUALITY
Yes I am spiritual. I believe in the Almighty God. As a believer, my decisions and way of life is based upon my core beliefs, principles and values from the Word of God. I pray

daily and throughout the day for guidance and understanding in all areas of life. Anything that I do, must be aligned with my spirit so that I can be at peace with my Heavenly Father.

FINANCES

I have always been financially savvy. I write out my financial goals (personal and business), budget and action steps each year as well as review on an as needed basis. Staying on track and remaining disciplined helps me maintain my financial goals. Another key element that keeps me accountable with finances, is being conscious about what I spend my money on. My financial goals mirror my values and beliefs. To maximize my fun and stretch my finances, I search for local activities that are either free or reduced costs through social media, libraries, eventbrite, meetup, word of mouth and organizations of interest. I look for opportunities to volunteer that align with things I love to do. I am a couponer and look for bargains before making any type of purchase. If I cannot get an upfront discount, I look for discounts on the backend from referring or affiliate marketing.

RELATIONSHIPS

I surround myself with people who can appreciate who I am. I am willing to compromise on things in relationships that will stretch me and promote growth. Relationships are important to keep healthy and thriving that's why I nurture the people in my life on a regular basis. I set aside time each day to show that I care for them.

CAREER & BUSINESS

It is imperative to maintain balance when it comes to business and other areas of life. Business in and of itself can be very demanding and take over your life so easily. In order to gain some balance, I had to learn to set boundaries.

Although it is a simple concept, it took me some time to get a good handle on it. I learned to schedule and plan out everything to be sure that I remain balanced and on task. I have personal and professional planning that I do in two separate planners and utilize Google calendars which allows me to color code to keep everything organized. All my calendars are synced to my cell phone so that I can be kept abreast of my schedule at anytime. I also have set days for work and play.

ABOUT TRYNETTE
I am Trynette Lariba, founder of Curvy Fit Chicks. I am pleasant and love to connect with people. I am the friend in the group that tells it like it is! It's probably just a Scorpio thing. I love my curves and am on a mission to redefine the standards of health and wellness for the Curvy Woman. I am a mommy and business owner so trust that I understand that the, "struggle is real." Like many women, my adult life has been an on and off affair with getting fit. The realization that this must stop came last year after having a flip-over car accident that changed everything. No longer does inconsistency or excuses dwell here. I am a BEAST when it comes to getting fit. I am ever more committed, conscious, and clear about my fitness goals and focused on helping other Curvy Women identify their 'WHY' and 'HOW' to get and stay active.

Curvy Fit Chicks is a community of ambitious Curvy women who are:

Committed to their goals
Empowered to take control of their lives
Focused on being healthy in every area of life
Excited to see other women win

TRIUMPHS

FUN FACTS
I love learning languages and cultures
I am a traveler by nature
I am a Registered Nurse
I prefer Caribbean/African cuisine to American cuisine

Find Trynette at
Founder: Curvy Fit Chicks
Email: curvyfitchicks@gmail.com
FB Group: Curvy Fit Chicks Group
FB Group Link: bit.ly/curvyfitchicksgroup
FB: Curvy Fit Chicks
IG: curvy_fit_chicks
Twitter: Curvy Fit Chicks

LIFE BALANCE FOR THE WOMEN ON THE RISE

By Joi Grant

LIFE

Recently, I overcame a situation in my life that made me realize how much I cared about what others thought of me. Sadly a few years ago, I found myself in a life threatening and uncomfortable situation that led me to being a victim of domestic violence.

The man I dated, trusted and loved, broke me down mentally, physically and emotionally – let's just say that I am glad God healed me everywhere that I was broken. No longer do I replay the recording of his detrimental words of hate, jealously and despair, but instead tell myself how simply amazing I am.

Constantly, he would remind me of the low-income neighborhood I came from and how that made me a whore because I was from the Projects. His stereotypical behavior and words made me question my very existence and purpose on earth. One thing that I know for sure anyone can change and become better, and I found the strength to put the pieces to my life back together, and I am loving the transformation.

MIND & BODY

As a direct result of feeling isolated and as if nobody cared I decided that I would put my trust in The Lord. Telling the Lord all my struggles, issues and challenges relieved me a great deal. My new regimen consisted of rising early in the morning and making time for just God. Reading, praying and mediating is how I spent the first fifteen minutes of my day. Wonderful things began occurring, I became stronger and wiser. After all the things, I had endured and survived, the one person I valued, most told me, "We don't look at you the same way anymore."

With a delayed response, I said, "I no longer care what others think of me, I am FINALLY FREE!"

Presently, I renew my mind daily in God's word, which reminds me of all His promises that keep me on track.

SPIRITUALITY
Balance is monumental in life, and living because without it one can be all over the place and who has time for that as it is counterproductive. In my upcoming book, Create Your Own Lane, I speak about the importance of keeping your business and daily activities of living in a seamless balance. The most essential ingredients that matter most to me, and are strategically within planner's list of must have's, and to do list are centered around Faith, Family, Spiritual (Gods Time), Finances, Health, Business, Travel, and Education. Truly, I believe that these eight key principals (Faith, Family, Focus, Finances, Health, Business, Travel and Education keep me on track to achieving my goals, thus ensuring that I am balanced. My life is based on gratitude and asking God for guidance through my wellness journey of eating clean; both natural and spiritual foods; avoiding toxic people.

FINANCES
In the past, I struggled with financial balance and fear. Most recently, I had to have a, "Come to Jesus moment," where I sat me and my finances down and had a serious one on one to figure it all out. After analyzing my bills, receipts and miscellaneous spending, I was shocked after calculating it all that I only was left with $98.27 and that was for the month. WOW!

Presently, I am on track, saving more within my pension, for business and my girls education.

RELATIONSHIPS

In a deep conversation with my reality and the life I was offering my girls wasn't conducive to living, so it was a struggle, but by God's grace, I changed for the best. The transition wasn't always easy, but I would put money into my cabinets and refrigerator because it was empty since I spent too much money on buying expensive and unhealthy fast foods.

CAREER & BUSINESS

Learning to split my time between my girls, granddaughter, career and business is a balancing act all within itself. My business doesn't take a back seat either because it has its own schedule too, and I work it when it calls for it – which is daily. I only work on my business when I am not at work or with my daughters. Being present is a gift that God granted me and I take it serious.

ABOUT JOI

Mompreneur, GlamMa, Woman of God, Entrepreneur, Author, Project Manager, Event Coordinator, Youth Mentor, Business Coach, Motivational Speaker and Survivor of Domestic Violence, I vow to live on purpose – because titles aren't as important as the work that must be done to reshape lives.

As an Author, Coach & Motivational Speaker, I speak to ignite thought, reshape minds and shift time – in order that women do what they were born to do. With all these titles, and life, I stay focused on the end results. My Vision Boards Workshops always helps my audience find their voice while discovering innovative ways to Create Your Own Lane-simply to remain sane. You can connect with me on www.JoiGrant.com and within my Facebook Group called Create Your Own Lane.

Find Joi at
Instagram: create_your_own_with_joi
Facebook group: Create your own lane

LIFE BALANCE FOR THE WOMEN ON THE RISE

By Yadlynd Cherubin-Eide

LIFE
I try my best to stay focused on my ultimate professional and family goals. As a full time Licensed Realtor and Real Estate investor there is so much information available about me online, I realize that it is very easy for people to pass judgments and make assumptions about who they think I am. I realize and understand that it is important to be true to myself and what I stand for.

When I decided to leave my career as a Human Resources administrator to focus on real estate, people thought I was crazy. That reaction really was a source of motivation for me and helped propel me to where I am now.

MIND & BODY
One thing that I can say is that I always strive for a healthy life balance. We as woman wear so many hats and play so many roles in life that a healthy balance is so necessary. As an entrepreneur, I find myself working longer hours and harder to maintain my family business. As a result, I make sure that I set aside time for my family and myself. As a mother of two amazing boys, I plan yearly vacations that we all enjoy. I organize family dinners and events to get everyone together. My husband and I set aside time for just us. I also squeeze in time for Zumba and Pilates classes at my local gym and meetings/ lunches with my close friends. All of these things help me create a healthy balance of all that is important to me.

SPIRITUALITY
I'm very spiritual. Before stepping out of bed, I give thanks and praise to God. I ask for guidance and direction for my family and business. I consult with God before entering deals and business ventures.

FINANCES

I am a big planner. Real estate income fluctuates, so I am sure to discuss our family financial short term and long term goals with my husband and accountant yearly. My husband and I set up our retirement accounts and NYS 529 college savings accounts for our boys. It is also important to set up life insurance plans. It is very important that you and your partner are on the same page financially. I also plan our family vacation sometimes a year in advance to get really good deals.

RELATIONSHIPS

I make a conscious decision to spend quality time with the ones I love. I have counsel with my sisters to discuss our lives and how we can improve our friendships and relationships. We discuss the legacy that we want to create for our children and future generations. We have family gatherings, so that we all stay connected and are involved in each other lives.

CAREER & BUSINESS

The real estate business is a demanding, yet flexible business. One of the reasons, I decided to focus on real estate full time after so many years, is because I wanted more time with my growing family. Real Estate provides me with the flexibility to make a great income, and it also allows me to be very involved in my community and activities with my children. I would encourage any mom who is considering a career change to look into the real estate industry. I absolutely love what I do, and I can say for sure that my family is so much happier with my career choice.

ABOUT YADLYND

Yadlynd Cherubin is a NYS Licensed Real Estate Salesperson and Team Leader of Legacy Group and Founder of Legacy Group Properties inc. With over 15 years of experience in the NYC/LI real estate market, she offers her real estate clients an exceptional blend of enthusiasm, dedication and expertise in real estate. Specialties includes:

- Real Estate investing
- Buyer's Agent
- Listing Agent
- Relocation
- Short-Sale
- Property Management

Find Yadlynd at
Facebook: https://www.facebook.com/yadlynd.cherubineide
Instagram: https://www.instagram.com/yadlynd/

Harvest Time

It is with joy and jubilee that I come before you, Heavenly Father, giving thanks for the many blessings that you are bestowing upon me. Thank you for the harvest you are manifesting in my life because I have been obedient to your word. You said sow, and I sowed; you said pray, and I prayed; you said trust and I had faith. Your word says obedience is better than sacrifice (1Samuel 15:22), you say test me and see if I won't pour you out a blessing too large to contain (Malachi 3:10). Thank you that you are not a man, and you cannot lie. Thank you for a time of harvest.

Maureen Smith

Now he who supplies seed to the sower and bread for food will also supply and increase your store of seed and will enlarge the harvest of your righteousness. 2 Corinthians 9:10

CONCLUSION
And So It Begins
By Marsha Guerrier

Now is the moment that you have come to the decision point in your journey. We have empowered you with tools and the inspiration that you need to succeed in finding that balanced feeling you have been yearning for. It is up to you to take action to make the necessary shifts to achieve fulfillment and happiness or **SLIDE BACK** into your old routine and make no progress.

Just like our authors and writers, your life was designed to be unique. Once you've become more connected with your values and putting your priorities in order, you will begin to see that life can feel balanced even during adversity. It comes from within. As you **GROW** to be a better individual, your family, friends and colleagues will take notice and soon after will be inspired to transform as well.

How will you implement what you've learned? We've shared other women's stories and hope that you too will share your story of triumph with others to help motivate and inspire someone else. Remember that the goals you've set for your life are yours and **ONLY** yours. You must remain steadfast in your transformation even when the tough gets going, keep in mind the going gets tough.

Know that without mapping out your goals and creating a plan you can stick with, you are setting yourself up for failure. **FAILURE IS NOT AN OPTION**. When one door closes, another door opens, so be prepared to reorganize, reprioritize and revise.

We are Women on the Rise, there is no ceiling, keep rising. Join our community of supportive and encouraging women that want to see you grow at:
www.facebook.com/groups/wearewomenontherise/.

And so it begins, our mentors and coaches are there to work with you when you are ready.

ABOUT THE AUTHORS

Marsha Guerrier

Marsha Guerrier is a personal and professional development coach and the founder and CEO of Women on the Rise NY, Inc. a small business consulting firm. She is also a mompreneur with a full-time career in the financial technology industry spanning over 20 years working for Fortune 500 and startup firms. She currently is working as a Software Analyst. Marsha has also founded the Yva Jourdan Foundation a non-profit organization dedicated to helping families with special needs and has served as the Executive Director for over 8 years. Marsha holds a BS in Business, Management and Economics. She is a two time recipient of the State Assembly of New York's Women of Distinction Award for both her work with the Yva Jourdan Foundation and Women on the Rise NY, Inc.

Marsha is dedicated to the theory that coaching is both a life tool and a business tool. As a strategic, visionary thinker, she has a passion for inspiring people, at all levels, to optimize their full potential while maintaining a focus on goal setting, reflection and life balance. Her clients include Authors, Beauty Professionals, Caterers, Child Care Professionals, Coaches, Floral Designers, Realtors and more.

Marsha supports women as they learn to organize, prioritize and develop strategies for their personal and professional life. Through Women on the Rise NY, Inc. she provides 1 on 1 and group mentoring, a business mastermind group, and an annual Forum & Expo. She is available for panel discussions and workshops on Goals Setting, Transforming and Mastering the Mind and Using Fear to Motivate You to Succeed.

Ohilda Holguin

Rev. Ohilda Holguin is a High Priestess, and Associate Pastor of the Sanctuary of the Beloved. She is a Best-Selling Author, Speaker, Spiritual Business Coach, Radio Personality, and Entrepreneur. Known as the "Self-Discovery Coach", she has a private holistic wellness practice, **"Well by Ohi"**, and is COO of Elite Sales Consulting Group. She is a recurring host on Sistah Chat Radio Show, and co-owner of Sistah Chat Global Media™. Currently she is an EPIC Ambassador for Coach, Speak, & Serve™, an Ambassador for LatinaVIDA™, Ambassador for Beautiful Money™, and is a power partner with the Business of WE.

Ohi is an imaginative and creative visionary who is a source of inspiration to most. Ingenious, enthusiastic, inventive, and extremely perceptive. She is strong on initiative, new ideas and insights. She is noted for her innate ability to inspire and encourage others. She is dedicated to empowering business owners, executives, and women by teaching them to stand in their own power. Ohi has spent her entire life studying health, wellness, counseling, meditation, and spirituality. She has devoted her life to helping others. A spiritual awakening has led Ohi to re-commit her life to helping others heal, become more enlightened, and expand their consciousness. Now in addition to helping businesses grow, Ohi empowers people to heal themselves by learning to speak their truth, listen their spirit, connect to energy, and love themselves unconditionally.

Ohilda Holguin is a certified Holistic Life Coach, obtaining her coaching certification from Compass Schoobl of Coaching. She is also certified in Reiki from the New York Open Center, and Level 1 & 2 EFT Universe certified Facilitator who uses heart-centered tapping to help you feel safer in your body, relationships, and in the world. Ohi is also certified in Abhyanga Oil Massage through S.A.M.A. She is a co-author of H.O.P.E: Hearing Other People's Experiences by Dr. Veronie Lawrence and is currently working on Driven Success by Aprille Franks-Hunt as well as her own book.

She holds a Bachelor of Psychology & Business, a Master of Education, and is currently working on her Ayurveda Health Coach Certification at Sacred Stone Academy of Massage & Ayurveda.

To find out more about her services and/or join her VIP email list please visit:
www.Ohilda.com or www.elitesalesconsultinggroup.com.

Kymberley Clemons-Jones

Kymberley's life has always been dedicated to helping women and youth see themselves as the Creator sees them; as praise-worthy. Kymberley currently serves as Pastor of Valley Stream Presbyterian Church in Valley Stream, New York. She is a loving and nurturing pastor to both her parishioners and to those who have come to work under her leadership in ministry.

She is the founder of the Community Healing and Caring Center Inc., a nonprofit organization focused on family cohesion, community building and restoration. The W.A.N.T.E.D. Project, a mentoring program for young men 12-18 years old, is flourishing in New York and in Ghana, West Africa and seeks to tell its participants that they are worthy, accountable, named, thankful, empowered and determined.

Kymberley is the principal of Restored Life, where she coaches individuals and groups in the areas of spirituality and emotional health and wellness. Through her coaching practice, she offers a personalized regimen of spiritual discipline techniques and the Emotional Freedom Techniques (EFT – Tapping).

Kymberley is the author of "Cured But Not Healed: How to Experience Deeper Faith on Your Journey with God", which was chosen by the 800,000 member United Methodist Women's Organization Reading Program for 2016. She is an international co-author of "The Women's Guide to Holistic Health and Wellness" amongst others. Kymberley will be releasing her newest work, a book of poetry, called "The Flourishing of Her Soul" within the next few weeks.

You can find Rev. KC Jones at kcjones@restorationlifecoach.com or thewantedproject.mentoring@gmail.com.

Vanessa Lindley

Vanessa A. Lindley is the CEO of The Lindley Consulting Group LLC. She is a dynamic speaker, trainer, coach and author with over 20 years experience in the financial services and leadership development arena.

Vanessa is an alumnus of the Goldman Sachs 10K Small Business program, a certified **Minority and Women Owned Business with the City and State of New York and** a licensed Real Estate Broker. She's been a State Farm Agent, where she held licenses in all lines of insurance, Series 6 and 63 and has owned and managed over $2 million in real estate.

As an author, Vanessa has written and contributed to several publications and curricula such as, "Breaking Free," "Realizing the American Dream," "Financial Coaching: Helping Clients Reach their Goals" and "Delivering Effective Financial Education for Today's Consumer." She is also the financial contributor for Women of More Magazine and the National Urban League.

As a nationally recognized leader she's worked with a diverse client base that include Citi, Chase, NeighborWorks America, the FDIC, National Urban League, the Congressional Black Caucus Foundation, Freddie Mac, State of New York Mortgage Association among other organizations. She's a frequent award recipient of including Community Leader of the Year, a finalist in FinCapDev mobile app design contest and "Flawless Facilitator" by the Goldman Sachs 10K Small Business Cohort.

Contact Vanessa Lindley
Website: LindleyConsultingGroup.com
Email: Vanessa@LindleyConsultingGroup.com
IG: FB: Twitter: @VanessaLindley

Donyshia Boston-Hill

Donyshia Boston-Hill, the CEO, of Keeper of the Brand Marketing & Digital Agency. Offering branded entertainment, marketing & digital solutions, unique programs and content for entertainment, sports, corporate, governmental developments, non-profit organizations and technology brands. Keeper of the Brand's current roster includes AARP, Battery Park City Authority, Nassau Community College, ZenoRadio, and Queens Library to name a few.

Donyshia has held leadership and management positions within several media and entertainment companies, including The New York Knicks, Madison Square Garden College Basketball tournaments, The Loud Digital Network, 101.9 RXP, 98.7 Kiss FM and HOT 97. During her tenure at HOT 97, Donyshia's vision and creativity was credited with leading the production team to the continuous growth of the iconic HOT 97 Summer Jam Concert and HOT 97 Summer Jam's Pre-Festival and Attraction. Boston-Hill held the position as President of the Hip-Hop Heart Foundation and Vice President of the Kiss Cares Foundation activating the stations community relations efforts.

Among her many honors, Donyshia has been recognized by RAB, BMI & MIW "Rising Through the Ranks". Donyshia has published articles in national magazines, been quoted in major publications, appeared on national television and radio, and has presented seminars on Marketing throughout the United States. She is a featured author of the books, The Fearless Living Experience, My Now for the Future Woman, The Professional Black Woman, and Life Balance for the Women On the Rise available at donyshiabostonhill.com.

You can also hear Donyshia Boston-Hill every Thursday

on Tower Talk Business Radio at 3pm on 90.3fm WHPC as co-host interviewing business leaders and industry experts. In her spare time, Donyshia is the Creative Director for Ice Princess NYC, a Special Events Planning, Invitation and Wedding Essentials company.

Donyshia is an alumna of both St. John's University and New York University and currently resides in New York with her husband and has two lovely children.

Monique Denton-Davis

Monique Denton-Davis is a passionate Life and Career Coach based in Long Island, New York. Raised in the same area, her passion for helping women began early on. Currently, Monique is the proud Founder & CEO of Embrace Your CAKE (Confidence, Attitude, Kindness, and Excellence) Career Coaching. She is also a dedicated Director, Trainer, and Recruiter who has worked for both corporate and nonprofit organizations.

For over two decades, Monique has held numerous leadership positions in the human resources field and utilizes all of that valuable know-how when working with her clients.

Monique's number one mission is to motivate women in all walks of life, encouraging them to embrace their C.A.K.E. and break through any obstacle with an unwavering sense of confidence. Nothing makes her happier than seeing people win and live the fulfilling life that they have always deserved.

Credentials:
Monique is certified in Human Resource Management, Diversity and Inclusion. Monique is also a certified Non-Violent Crisis Intervention Trainer and holds a Degree in Organizational Management.

Maureen Smith

Maureen Smith is a retired financial professional. She has held varied titles, leading and developing other professionals during her thirty-five plus years in the industry.

Her most coveted title however is that of mother of three adult children, grandmother (of three) and most recently great-grandmother. She is loves God, people, and life, striving daily to live it to the fullest.

A true believer in Christ, she is passionate about learning and teaching God's word. She lives to see women and children grow in the knowledge of God, and has taught in Children's Ministry for over twenty-five years, including teaching "teachers" how to minister to children. After the many years of teaching children God "promoted" or added to her sphere of influence women. She finds there is nothing more compelling that watching women and children claim their God given place in society as they learn how much God loves them and has a plan and purpose for their lives.

She currently leads a weekly women's Bible study, among the many other activities a retired person can enjoy.

Blessings

For I know the plans I have for you," declares the Lord, "plans to prosper you and not to harm you, plans to give you hope and a future.
Jeremiah 29:11

There is surely a future hope for you, and your hope will not be cut off.
Proverbs 23:18

He who was seated on the throne said, "I am making everything new! "Then he said, "Write this down, for these words are trustworthy and true."
Revelations 21:5

www.ingramcontent.com/pod-product-compliance
Lightning Source LLC
Chambersburg PA
CBHW070622300426
44113CB00010B/1623